# EISNER/MILLER

### A ONE-ON-ONE INTERVIEW
### CONDUCTED BY CHARLES BROWNSTEIN

**DARK HORSE BOOKS**™

**DIANA SCHUTZ**
**CHARLES BROWNSTEIN**
editors

**KATIE MOODY**
assistant editor

**CHRIS HORN**
**JASON HVAM**
digital production

**CARY GRAZZINI**
book design

**MIKE RICHARDSON**
publisher

Published by
Dark Horse Books
A division of Dark Horse Comics, Inc.
10956 SE Main Street
Milwaukie, Oregon 97222

darkhorse.com

First edition: May 2005
ISBN 1-56971-755-9

10 9 8 7 6 5 4 3 2 1

PRINTED IN CANADA

# INTRODUCTION

Will Eisner and I argued a lot.

My dear friend and honored colleague — hell, the man was, and remains, one of my most precious idols — died before this book saw print. I'm just getting started with the mourning.

I moved to my home, New York City, in the mid-1970s. I got to meet the Master pretty soon. I learned much from him, but almost always through argument.

My friend Will Eisner liked an argument.

There's no other way to paint it: It was New York. It was publishing. That kinda meant Jews. And Jews love an argument.

Jews created comic books, as best I can tell. Two Jews created Superman. Another created Batman. And a certain Jacob Kurtzberg, who renamed himself Jack Kirby ... well, don't get me started.

He never let up, Will didn't. Not in his own work, and not in conversation. He dropped his *Contract with God* on my field like an atom bomb — creating a movement toward permanence that has, magically but inevitably, persisted.

Old Will, he'd always push me and push me and teach me about how I couldn't possibly have balloon tails cross each other, and such and such. He was, arguably, right just about all of the time.

What you're about to read is the climax of our several-decade debate.

I'll bet he wins.

Frank Miller
New York 2005

# 1.·····

# INTENT

*The year is 2002. In the backyard of Will Eisner's suburban Florida home, late afternoon fades to evening. Will Eisner and Frank Miller are sitting at a lawn table beside Eisner's pool in the stuffy afternoon heat of Tamarac in May. Ann Eisner is preparing dinner inside.*

**MILLER:** One of the things I like about comics is that they are part of pop culture. I like being square in the mix of things like music and all of that. I don't see us as derivative *of them*, I see us more as participants in that arena. For instance, when I jumped back into doing superheroes again recently, some of the biggest sources I had for material were the absolutely latest happenings in fashion. It's on fire! They're doing crazy stuff in fashion.

..........................................................................................

**Opposite: Eisner's illustration, created especially for this volume, of the interview setting and its participants. © 2005 Will Eisner**

**EISNER:** We separate there, because you are more connected to what's going on. I'm still reporting, telling stories about the past. Diana Schutz beats me in the head about that because she says I ought to stop telling those stories and — what do you say? — expose myself. I tell stories.

**MILLER:** I tell stories too, Will.

**EISNER:** I know you do, I know you do *[Miller laughs]*. But I'm talking about — you're connected with the main flow. I talk about yesterday.

> "Part of the real difference between our intentions is that right now what I perceive as your goal in the work is technically drama. Whereas I'm still completely mad over *melodrama*."

**MILLER:** I think I probably fit more street theater in my stories. I jump all over what's currently going on. I don't know. I think there are central questions we're all facing as to *what* our intent is.

**EISNER:** Well, for instance, I talk to people about the institution of marriage. You've got no time for that, because the people you're talking to are not dealing with it. You're involved in the mainstream. You're right in there with the excitement of it, and you're aware of it. I'm talking about, in *A Contract with God,* man's relationship to God. The guy who's reading your stuff doesn't give a shit about man's relationship to God. He wants to see whether Marvin kills that son of a bitch or doesn't kill that son of a bitch or whoever it is he's adopted to assassinate or kill or beat up. We're talking to different people. *You're aware of it.*

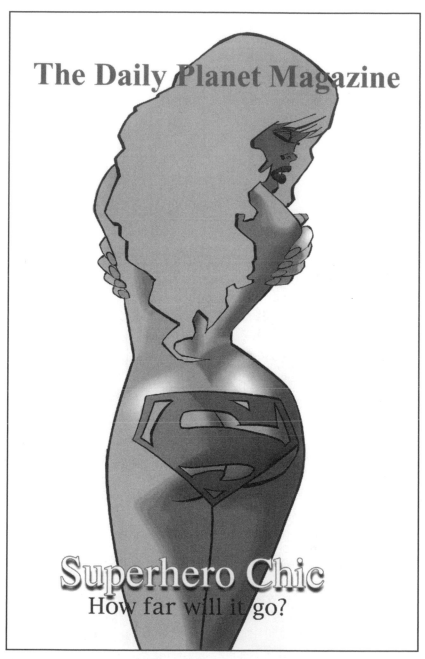

Miller is entranced by the "sense of complete absurdity" inherent in current times. From volume 2 of *Batman: The Dark Knight Strikes Again* [or *DK2*]. © 2002 DC Comics, Inc.

**MILLER:** Really, that was an unfair characterization. My stuff deals with that, too. It's more than pandering. My stuff is just more operatic than what you're currently doing. I'm not going to go into a lengthy defense of the complexity of my work, but my stories aren't just about people killing each other.

**EISNER:** Well, maybe I misjudged or mischaracterized. I don't get a chance to evaluate my stuff myself. I've never had the chance to characterize myself, so I don't know. I know that I'm talking about things that have very limited resonance. I'm not as involved as you are or as aware as you are of current interests. I may be *aware* of it, but I don't want to be involved with it.

**MILLER:** See, part of what I find entrancing about current times is the sense of complete absurdity. I guess if I were to look for an example in film of something I find particularly refreshing and inspiring, it would be Stanley Kubrick's old movie *Dr. Strangelove,* because he showed you things spinning out of control at such velocity. And he was able to hit so many different angles of what was going on in really a rather short movie. And he did so *brilliantly.* I guess that's where I'm aiming.

**Eisner's reader "has a lot of real-life experience." From "Moment of Glory," a wordless short printed in *Dark Horse Maverick 2001.* © 2001 Will Eisner**

Part of the real difference between our intentions is that right now what I perceive as your goal in the work is technically drama. Whereas I'm still completely mad over *melodrama.* I like romance. I like the Big. Broad. Strokes. *A Family Matter,* to me, was one of your most finely attuned climaxes because of the ending and how it was treated — and really how murderous you were at the end of that book.

**EISNER:** I was angry. There were a couple of books that came out of what I was angry about. *Invisible People* ... I was in a rage.

What I was talking about is the question of *who* your reader is. Your reader is the guy who is very much involved with the business of living the way you are. He's as frightened and confused as you ... know he is, and you say to him, "Hey, wait a minute ..."

**MILLER:** So, in other words, your reader is you.

**EISNER:** My reader is people like me. The best example I give is the sixty-year-old guy who just had his wallet stolen on the subway. That's my reader. My reader has a lot of real-life experience. He thinks maybe that God's full of shit. He feels like an ant. We're struggling with the demons inside of us. Each of us has a demon inside of us that we're dealing with.

**MILLER:** And they change shape across time.

**EISNER:** They do.

# 2.·····
# FORMAT

**MILLER:** How long are we going to be controlled by the fact that a long time ago an old guy folded a newspaper in half, twice, and gave us an ugly format that we've been stuck with?

**EISNER:** Well, you're going to be stuck with that as long as the manufacturing process is the same. As long as you're on paper, you're going to be stuck with that.

**MILLER:** The pamphlet stinks so much. The periodical nature of comics is so wrong. It's not just that it's bad for commerce, it's terrible for the art, too. People have to make the stuff too dense to make it worth $2.50, but at ten cents it made sense. Now it costs over two bucks to get, and it's only twenty pages of story, and [artists] have to put nine panels on a page.

.......................................................................

**Opposite: The 32-page "pamphlet" — an endangered species?** *Cover art © 1997 Frank Miller, Inc.*

**EISNER:** That's a major problem in this medium right now: that there isn't really accessible, low-priced material. A 32-page book is now $2.25 — who's going to pay that much for it?

**MILLER:** It makes no sense. It's only tradition that keeps it alive.

**EISNER:** Although … I was just sent one of the big boxes of DC comics, and it included an elongated book.

> ### "The pamphlet stinks so much.
> ### The periodical nature of comics is so wrong."

**MILLER:** They got the idea from *300.*

**EISNER:** They did?

**MILLER:** It's called the *widescreen* format or something.

**EISNER:** I think that's great — somebody made an effort to go beyond the shape. I like the classic shape myself because I think my reader is used to that and it's accommodating to my reader's way of reading.

**MILLER:** I guess my instincts are eventually to try to go horizontal with it on a regular basis. To me, the reason most books are vertical is because they're prose, and we don't want to read lines of prose that are too long. But the natural way to read comics is horizontally. My feeling is the fewer tiers the better, and the wider the tiers the better. It's basically a page that looks something like a Sunday strip but reads horizontally.

I found when I did *300* that there was something that felt so much more organic about it, because as humans we tend not to look up and down so much as we do side to side.  The horizontal image, I find, is much better for capturing landscape and detail.

**EISNER:**  I remember *300* very well, because I took some time to study it.  I looked at it two or three times because I was admiring what you were doing there.  But you were breaking not so much the pattern of the geometric size that you're stuck with, but within that pattern you were moving the eye and developing space — the same reason I drop panel [borders].  You were engaging the reader in space, which is a totally different thing.  Remember, the reason comics are what they are is because all books are built that way.  When you start reading as a child, you're reading a book exactly the way a comic book is printed today.

**MILLER:**  You've been fighting format yourself.  Most of your books are now 6x9 [inches] rather than the classic comic book size.  The classic

*300*'s "widescreen" format effect.  Each comics-size issue was made up of double-page spreads, which became single, horizontal pages in the hardcover book collecting the series. © *1998, 1999 Frank Miller, Inc.*

comic book size is just plain awful.  It's ugly; it's neither here nor there.
It's not big enough to be an art book.

**EISNER:** The difference between 7x10 and 6x9 is that 6x9 has a greater
intimacy, in my opinion, and it also, again, brings the book within the
range of what the adult reader regards as a *book*.  The adult reader doesn't
like to read a 7x10 book because it's like a comic book.  But he likes to
look at a book that's 6x9 because all his novels are 6x9.

**MILLER:**     There's also the convenience of carrying it.  When I
was getting ready to go to the airport, I was thinking, "God, I want
something to read.  The newspapers won't last me." And I was looking
and I thought, "I haven't read any comics in a long time." I was finishing
up a job, and I never read comics while I'm in the heat of it.  And there
was a great Charles Burns book, but it was too damn big to carry, and I
caught myself in that moment as a reader.  To me that was one of those
moments confirming that formats really are important.

> "Essentially, we are slaves to people's
> Mylar plastic bags.  And that's insane!"

**EISNER:** Those are factors, yeah.  It's a package.  But, again, you and I
have grown up with paper.  To this day, when I get a book that I've just
published, I still open it up and smell it.

**MILLER:** Yeah, it's like a new car.

**EISNER:** Yeah, yeah, yeah!  It has a "new book" smell to it.  It comes
from the time I was working at cleaning presses in a print shop.

We're dealing with a public perception of what it is readers know and
understand, and that's the wonderful thing for guys like you and me,

because we've got something to tear apart. In order to get readership, we have to stay within the parameters of what somebody wants to read.

**MILLER:** But, also, there's a historical stupidity that makes me nuts. Again, we're dealing with a newspaper folded twice. That's not the limit of printing anymore; that's a tradition. Essentially, we are slaves to people's Mylar plastic bags. And that's insane! That's suicide, in the long run. We can't keep playing to that group to the point that we won't even stretch the form and actually get some decent dimensions. Either bigger or smaller — just something new.

The smaller size really does offer intimacy. I think one of the reasons that you're drawn to it, if I can try to speak for you, is that you really do regard this as first and foremost a literary form, and that format marries it closer to prose.

I believe that one has a different relationship with a smaller book than one does with a large one. An art book is almost a communal thing. If you're around, you can see it too. With *A Contract with God,* it's just you and the reader. You're in the room with the guy and no one else is there. I like big and I like small; I just wish that those shelves in comic book shops looked a lot different. I wish they had all kinds of different formats instead of having the single ugliest format dominate.

**EISNER:** Right on. I agree with you. It's one of the few times in this whole discussion that I'll *totally* agree with you and not change a single word *[Miller laughs]*. I'm not repelled by the oddness of size. If someone comes out with a book that's 12x14, I feel fine, that's okay. It just doesn't have the intimacy.

**MILLER:** The comic book size is just so awkward. In fact, talking about printing, they waste three inches of paper at the top of everything they do in the comic book format. The paper is actually taller and thinner.

**EISNER:** That's right: the average page size coming off the press is 8½x11, actually. Twenty-two inches is the width of standard paper. There are various reasons. Again, you and I are both seeking to make a contact with the reader. In your *Sin City* books the black-and-white provides an intimacy: you're being talked to directly. To me, color is intrusive. To me, color is like a major symphony orchestra playing behind Edith Piaf.

**MILLER:** You're talking about color, and I'd like to pursue that a bit. I'm lucky to work with a pretty amazing colorist. I find that when I'm working with Lynn [Varley], it's just a completely different project than it is in black-and-white.

**EISNER:** *300* was smashing color; it sang. But then again, your style that you employed accommodated color. It was operatic.

**MILLER:** When Lynn and I work, it really is as artists in collaboration. I trade part of my authorship for a completely different effect. I give her no direction. But it is a very different kind of comic book.

> "To me, color is intrusive.
> To me, color is like a major symphony
> orchestra playing behind Edith Piaf."

**EISNER:** It really isn't a comic book; it's a book. I consider *300* a book.

**MILLER:** You immediately made a musical reference when you mentioned color. It's funny that you'd do that, because I think of things like sound and temperature when I'm working with Lynn. I really am setting it up. I'm essentially the director, but I'm sure as hell not the cinematographer.

Color's such a powerful arsenal, and there's no nice way to put this: it's one that's really not used much in our field with purpose. Everything's airbrushed and it's all so tight. Most comic books are kind of *brown* now, ever since computers came in. There's a joyous absurdity to superheroes that I think we could see enjoying itself more in most comics.

That said, you do see some really beautifully painted comics. They have them in Europe. And, of course, some of the limited color work that people like David Mazzucchelli, Chris Ware, and Dan Clowes obviously care about.

**EISNER:** I believe, by and large, color has been functionally used as a marketing tool. For example, in my classes the question always came up with page layout. People would ask how I composed a page, and I kept telling them that the page will compose itself. But this came once again from the major publishing house directive that says: Do me a book so that when you open it up, people will look at it and say, "Oh, I gotta buy this book." The page has to be *exciting*. Everybody should be on a splash page.

That always amused me that they referred to my first page as a *splash* page. I don't know why. I never used a splash, except once I had water on a page *[Miller laughs]*.

Anyway, the books are being designed now to be compelling as you open them up. They scream and yell. Content is not important at all. The big difference is the fact that if John Updike sits down and writes a book, he's not thinking, "Will this be in Bodoni or will it be in Cheltenham [two different typefaces]? Maybe we'll do Times-Roman!" He doesn't worry about the typeface he's using; he doesn't even think about it.

I believe color is used essentially as a packaging device, rather than as an integral storytelling device.

A *Spirit* "splash" page — on the waterfront.  First published December 11, 1949.
© *1949 Will Eisner*

**MILLER:** In *Sin City*, a number of times I've had fun stringing color in *specifically* as a narrative device, and only one color. In one case, there was one where it was simply the color of a woman's dress, with the obvious effect. Because it just showed off her figure constantly throughout the story.

> **"If you don't use color for a purpose, why waste the ink?**

**EISNER:** That was the one where her dress was red? *[Miller nods.]* It worked beautifully.

**MILLER:** It's amazing how it works. Color's a very powerful thing, and I hate to see it squandered. I think there should be more black-and-white books, not only because they can work very well, but if you don't use color for a purpose, why waste the ink?

# 3.....

# THE WALK
# THROUGH THE RAIN

**EISNER:** Black-and-white books demand content because they are *read*. As opposed to color, which is really absorbed porously *[laughs]*. It's not by accident that *A Contract with God* was sepia. I had a choice between doing it in one color, two colors.

**MILLER:** That was a dramatic decision. I remember when the book came out, it was almost a physical shock.

**EISNER:** That's exactly what I was trying to say. People say that you dream in brown, did you ever hear that? Psychologists will tell you that you dream in brown. But it was the only way of introducing color in a way that gave the book a tone. I felt it developed an intimacy between me and the reader, as if we were talking in hushed tones.

..........................................................................................................................

**Opposite: Both the intimacy of black-and-white — or, in the case of *A Contract with God*, sepia brown — and Eisner's larger lettering serve to draw the reader in closely. © 1978 Will Eisner**

**MILLER:** I'd like to dwell on *A Contract with God*. It really is a seminal piece of work. From the walk-in-the-rain opening, part of what really made that an affecting piece of work was that you lettered it big. It drew the reader in. Just a few words, very large lettering, almost the look of a children's book, even though the content was clearly not childlike. And as it got more complex, you were already in the door, so you had to deal with it as you read it. But it very much drew you in. You're walking with somebody in the rain.

**EISNER:** Oh, yeah, the walk through the rain.

**MILLER:** Not just the walk through the rain, but the mounting tension was really something.

**EISNER:** It's a pure theatrical device, which is not of my invention. You may have used it in some of your work.

**MILLER:** I did, in the first *Sin City* [*The Hard Goodbye*]. There's a scene that goes for about ten pages where I wanted to build as much tension as possible with the atmosphere of the rain. That was me saying, "This is where I'm going. I've been away from comics for two years, and I'm back." I sat down and did exactly what I wanted to do without thinking about it. That was my walk in the rain.

**EISNER:** I think I have a copy of that one on the shelf. *[Examines the book.]* This is great. There's real power here. I can hear the wind whistling. Without reading the text … as a [purely] visual thing you're evoking a feeling on the part of the reader. I can feel this rain, and I can hear the roar of the wind and the rain splashing in the gutter. And then suddenly the appearance of a face. All of a sudden it's beginning to take shape. I congratulate you.

**MILLER:** I did a lot of white paint on those pages, too.

**EISNER:** Did you? It looks like you did it on scratchboard.

**Miller's (and Marv's) walk in the rain, from *Sin City: The Hard Goodbye*. ©1992
*Frank Miller, Inc.***

........................................................................................................

**MILLER:** No, I did it on white board in layers. I ruled the brush lines in black, and then I came in with white.

**EISNER:** Did you draw the figure in first and then do the rest?

**MILLER:** Yes.

**EISNER:** That's the way I would do it. I'd draw the figure in full and then add the white.

**MILLER:** I tend to work from a pretty specific image and then degrade it.

**EISNER:**  Okay, you say "degrade" — you convert it.  This book I'm working on [*Fagin the Jew*] has a snow scene.  I finished the scene completely and then threw the splashes of snow on it.

**MILLER:**  Did you ever use liquid frisket?

**EISNER:**  What is it, a kind of rubber cement?

> "But the problem that you set for yourself creates the innovation."

**MILLER:**  It's essentially the same as rubber cement, but it's a little more fluid so you can really snap it from a brush.  I used a lot of it in *Family Values*.  The fun thing about that is that it's really got the art of accident, because you ink on top of the frisket and then pull off the ink, and you have no idea what it's gonna look like when it comes off.

**EISNER:**  Oh, yeah!  I've done that.  In one of the books, I did the title with rubber cement, painted in the letters, and then blacked over it and pulled off the rubber cement.  You get some very interesting effects.

**MILLER:**  Yeah.  I bought an old Johnny Craig EC [Entertaining Comics] job once that was on auction, and it was all set in the snow, and I went crazy trying to figure out how he did the snow without any white-out.  I had no idea you could do that.  It leaves a frighteningly clean board *[Eisner laughs]*.

**EISNER:**  I was always surprised to find, when I saw Milton Caniff's originals, that he used a lot of white paint.  The thing that intrigued me when I first saw Milton Caniff's work was his handling of snow.  He did a house in the snow with just a few black shadows and a window, and you knew it was a house in the snow.

"SAINT PATRICK," THEY CALL HIM BUT IT'S JUST A NICKNAME. THE POPE HASN'T GOTTEN AROUND TO MAKING IT OFFICIAL. NOT YET, ANYWAY.

THE ROARK FAMILY HAS OWNED SIN CITY SINCE THE DAYS OF WAGON TRAINS AND SIX-GUNS. OVER THE GENERATIONS THEIR MILLIONS HAVE GROWN TO BILLIONS. THEY'RE KIND OF LIKE OUR OWN ROYAL FAMILY.

THIS PARTICULAR GENERATION PRODUCED A UNITED STATES SENATOR, A STATE ATTORNEY GENERAL--AND PATRICK HENRY ROARK.

CARDINAL ROARK.

BACK IN SCHOOL THE SISTERS WOULD NEVER SHUT UP ABOUT HIM. MAN OF THE CLOTH. WAR HERO IN THE MEDICAL CORPS. PHILANTHROPIST. EDUCATOR. COULD'VE BECOME PRESIDENT BUT HE CHOSE TO SERVE GOD.

AND ALONG THE WAY HE JUST HAPPENED TO BECOME THE MOST POWERFUL MAN IN THE STATE. HE'S BROUGHT DOWN MAYORS AND GOTTEN GOVERNORS ELECTED.

AND HERE HE'S GOING TO GET KILLED IN THE NAME OF A DEAD HOOKER.

I'M GETTING USED TO THE IDEA.

MORE AND MORE I'M LIKING THE SOUND OF IT.

**More rain in the town without pity.** ©*1992 Frank Miller, Inc.*

**Eisner's snow scene from *Fagin the Jew*: the snow was splashed on over the completed drawing.** © *2003 Will Eisner*

**MILLER:** He also had a way of implying texture that was pretty shocking. When I was putting together *300*, I was trying to figure out how to imply the texture of the helmets. I didn't want to do ornate detail, but I wanted them to feel like they were metal and they'd been on blocks the entire time. I was wondering what to do, and I looked at a Caniff *Terry and the Pirates* daily [newspaper strip] from the war [World War II], and there was a helmet there. I swear he must have inked the thing in about ten seconds, and it was perfect. A little stipple and it was there.

**EISNER:** He was good.

**MILLER:** The whole thing about the first *Sin City* is that I was rediscovering the love of drawing on that job. I had absolutely no boss, and it was the first thing I completely did from head to toe by myself.

**EISNER:** That is pure Caniff: good basic drawing with an unlimited amount of black. It's courageous. As a matter of fact, that's what students used to refer to as *courage*. They used to ask, "Where did you get the courage to do all that black?" It's because you have a good, strong underlying drawing. It's good draftsmanship here.

**MILLER:** The rain scene was one of two scenes where I first got the idea of simply not thinking about the number of pages. For me it was like I'd just stepped out of the cave into the morning.

> ## "Dealing with time in this medium is one of the key problems."

**EISNER:** I know how you feel. *A Contract with God* was the one where I finally came back and said, "To hell with this! It'll be 200 pages." But the problem that you set for yourself creates the innovation. *The Spirit* splash pages were the result of a problem. I didn't wake up one morning and say, "I'm going to do a splash page." It was a problem. I had a cover that was dropped into a newspaper, and I had to compete with everything else for the reader's attention. And I had another problem: I only had seven pages to tell the story, and I had to get the reader quickly into it. So the splash page came from that.

But the question of time ... dealing with time in this medium is one of the key problems. There are several things that this medium is basically unable to deal with. One is sound, so we use balloons. The other is time. We can't deal with time.

**MILLER:** Well, that's where all the fun tricks come in.

**EISNER:** That's where all these things happen. That's where you can afford to take four pages for a rain scene leading me up to the character that you want me to see coming out of the rain. Motion is another thing we have a problem with. We have to imply motion.

A *Spirit* splash page, allowing readers quick entry to the story.
© 1949 Will Eisner

**MILLER:** When it comes to motion, one of the things I love about comics is that you're free to exaggerate motion.

**EISNER:** You do that very well. Your cars really move *[Miller chuckles]*.

**MILLER:** But we got sidetracked. I want to get back to the point about your lettering in *A Contract with God*. It was quite powerful.

**EISNER:** It was interesting, lettering that book. I threw away about thirteen pages of that book. I had originally set it in type, and I looked at it and looked at it, and thought, "The hell with it — I'm going back to balloons!"

That brings up a very interesting bit of comics history, which may be worth injecting here. Somewhere around the middle thirties the newspaper syndicates decided they wanted to improve the quality of comics, and so they hired good illustrators like Alex Raymond. The idea was to bring in good people. Then just before the war, there was a newspaper in town, the *New York Compass*, that started a strip called *Barnaby*, and all the balloons were done in typeset. Because suddenly the struggle was about what to do about balloons — this terribly impossible device that we've stuck with — and they had to do something. This was an effort to add "quality."

**MILLER:** I'm signing my death warrant here, but I've gotta say that Hal Foster was wrong.[1]

**EISNER:** Well, Hal Foster was Hal Foster. He was not wrong, he was just Hal Foster *[laughter]*. I'll discuss balloons with you. The syndicates brought in great illustrators. Hal Foster was one, Alex Raymond was another, and there were a few other great pen-and-ink illustrators who were brought in to do comic strips. The idea was, let's get quality. Their idea of quality was better artwork. But the lettering in the balloons was

---

[1] Miller is referring to Foster's lack of dialogue balloons in *Prince Valiant*.

**The implied motion of Miller's gravity-defying cars, from _Sin City: Family Values_.**
© _1997 Frank Miller, Inc._

................................................................................................

something else again. Some said, "The hell with you, I'm doing my own balloons." Like Al Capp, whose letters were very, very large and really shouted. Just like Al. When Al Capp laughed, the whole building shook. When he talked, he talked _loud._

**MILLER:** I've always heard he was a handful.

**EISNER:** Oh, he was. The point is, there was an effort to do something about the balloons. The balloons have always been a problem, and they still are today. It's something I've been thinking about and struggling with myself. It seems that one of the great inhibitions in this business, the thing that's keeping adult readers away from us, is the balloon. When readers open a book and they see balloons, they then close it because it's a comic book. If there are no balloons, they'll buy the book.

**MILLER:** I think that might be changing.

**EISNER:** I hope so.

**MILLER:** The balloons are so precious — I mean that in a *good* way.

**EISNER:** Well, it's the only way to deal with a spoken word.

**MILLER:** It's interesting that you mention there was a move to do that, because from time to time comics have employed type. Almost exclusively type and almost always to disastrous effect.

**EISNER:** Harvey Kurtzman did it for years.

**MILLER:** Kurtzman got rid of it.

**EISNER:** No, he didn't. He used type in all of his balloons. He also used the umbilical balloons, which I hate. I used to argue for hours with Harvey. I said, "Harvey, you're going to ruin this business." He couldn't see it that way.

**Al Capp's hand-lettering "shouted." From *Li'l Abner*.**
© *1949 United Feature Syndicate, Inc.*

**So-called "umbilical" balloons, from Kurtzman and Elder's *Goodman Beaver*.**
*© 1961, 1962 Harvey Kurtzman and Will Elder*

**Eisner eschews balloons altogether in this story from *Last Day in Vietnam*, without sacrificing clarity. © 2000 Will Eisner**

The war's end opened a new era in the stock market. Trading was now becoming more sophisticated. There even were days when a million shares were traded. One or two houses were starting mutual funds, and more pension funds were enlarging their stock portfolios.

The Arnheim Company still catered to small holders -- widows, retirees and old-line family estates.

An example of Eisner's later efforts to integrate the "more adult" look of typesetting with traditional hand-lettered balloons, from *The Name of the Game*. © 2001 Will Eisner

**MILLER:**  It's almost like either you decide or you don't that there's an article of faith that there's not more than one exchange per panel.

**EISNER:**  A balloon is supposed to be an integral part of the action. When you have type strung across, with umbilicals strung all back and forth, that has no connection with the action at all.  But that was a phenomenon.  One of the phenomena with this business was an attempt to lift the level of *quality* of the comics by introducing typesetting.

**MILLER:**  Remember when Gil Kane did it?  Boy, did it not work.

**EISNER:**  No, it didn't.  Type has a sterility.

**MILLER:**  It's cold, and there's something about it being type that causes a person to overwrite.  There aren't enough words here — I'll put some more in!

**EISNER:**  Typesetting is a problem with me.  I have to do something with it to soften it up.

**MILLER:**  I have a real problem with it, too.  The only place where I think I might play with it is in sound effects, because there's something so artificial about it that I *want* it to be wrong.

**EISNER:**  What I'm doing with it now … in *The Name of the Game* I really went all out trying to develop a combination with typesetting that may work.  Really, it may attract the adult reader who's grown up with type and regards comics as a cheesy thing but illustrations as a legitimate thing.  I'm trying to integrate them.  So I'm using typesetting in that book to deal with time-changes and historical background and so forth. I don't know how well it'll work.  I haven't seen the sales figures on that book, and I have no way of knowing how well the book has done so far. I got good reviews in France, however.

Well, so much for balloons.  I think balloons are still a continuing problem.

# 4.·····

# CREATIVE
# PROBLEMS

**MILLER:** I think maybe our approaches are just different. I look at some of those things that people regard as our "problems," and I kinda want to shove their faces in them. I want bigger sound effects that really scream *comic books* right in their face.

**EISNER:** Frank, that's the wonderful thing about problems. Don't take problems away, because in order to deal with problems you invent things. You're dealing with problems; that's what makes your work what it is. What you regard as a problem is the ennui of the established norms.

**MILLER:** And here's something that really bothers me: the reverence a segment of the audience has for its own childhood, where we do so much derivative work because people want it to be "real." I've got reality all day long. Doing realism in comics is really saying we are the poor man's film.

**EISNER:** You're talking about photorealism like [Jim] Steranko did?

**MILLER:** His stuff is actually more abstract than a lot of the stuff that's coming out now.

**EISNER:** He did a series … very photorealistic stuff that looked like he had taken photographs and photocopied them.

**MILLER:** Yeah, *Chandler.*

**EISNER:** It was a very courageous effort, but I think it lost humanity.

**The "bigfoot" cartooning style of *DK2*. From volume 1. © 2001 DC Comics, Inc.**

**MILLER:** As time goes by, I find myself more and more in love with stuff that's closer to bigfoot cartooning. I want people's sweat to be *flying* off their heads when they're upset. It's something comics can do.

**EISNER:** That works when you have something to say. That's the joy and the beauty of [Robert] Crumb's work. It's real bigfoot, but it's more than just fun to read. He has something to say.

> **"I want people's sweat to be *flying* off their heads when they're upset."**

**MILLER:** Well, there's a lot of drawing underneath that.

**EISNER:** Yeah, he's a good artist.

**MILLER:** This is part of what draws me to the SPX [Small Press Expo] crowd. That is part of what it means to just discover the sheer joy of what a cartoon is and get past my study of anatomy and this and that. I avoided drawing cars for over a decade in comics. I just drew a bunch of boxes going up and down the street. But in *Sin City* I had to draw cars, because they're so important. I didn't draw a good car until I put it ten feet off the ground, because it became a *character* then. I practically give them faces now, they're so much fun to draw! And that's cartooning. An accurate rendering of a car going down the street looks, for one thing, like it's parked. Also, it takes away all the joy of cartooning.

**EISNER:** I'll buy that. I think that's a very good description of what a cartoon is. Taking a thing, a human being or a thing in motion, and capturing segments of a seamless flow of something, and selecting from the seamless flow those elements, those moments, that tell you the story of that whole.

**The "floating paper" motif used by Eisner in *The Spirit* ...**
*© 1949 Will Eisner*

... and later co-opted by Miller in *Daredevil*. From issue #170.
*© 1981 Marvel Comics*

**MILLER:** One of the motifs I picked up from you really early on that I used all over *Daredevil* was the floating pieces of paper. Which don't exist in real life, but they tell you the air is there. They give you the wind. I was ordered to stop putting little bits of paper in the comics by [Jim] Shooter [Marvel's then editor-in-chief]. So the next issue had a ticker-tape parade *[laughter]*.

> "What we're doing constantly is seizing the reader by the lapel, bringing him up close, and saying, 'Look, I want you to know about what I'm telling you.'"

**EISNER:** Atmosphere and environment are terribly important to the telling of a story. The only way you're going to make contact with your reader is by referring to something that the reader can feel. I learned early that every reader knows what rain feels like. Every reader knows about heat. Every reader knows about cold. And every reader knows about little annoying things like flies and paper that move around us all the time. And those are devices that are very accessible. Everybody should use them. It doesn't have to be a piece of paper. It can be anything.

**MILLER:** What's really fun, I think, is when you find a piece of atmosphere or a detail, and you make it the graphic substance of the scene, and your character's moving through the rain or whatever. That can be just a wonderful drawing experience, and you can really make a scene people remember.

**EISNER:** Harvey Kurtzman labeled rain *Eisnershpritz!* I like the feeling of atmosphere. I like the feeling of gritty atmosphere and dust. In *Sin City* you accomplish that every once in a while. There's a feeling of dust when that car is going down the road and the lights are on. I feel the atmosphere. I know what's going on. You're reaching me there. What we're doing constantly is seizing the reader by the lapel, bringing him up close, and saying, "Look, I want you to know about what I'm telling you."

**MILLER:** This comes back to the question of black-and-white versus color. I really like working both ways, but it's a completely different experience — and it's when I'm working black-and-white where I feel more like I've got my hands on the lapels, because there's nobody else there. It was a real lesson for me in this Batman book [*Batman: The Dark Knight Strikes Again*] to learn that I can't let anybody else letter my work. Todd Klein did a gorgeous job, but …

**EISNER:** I agree. I do all my own lettering; I've been doing it for the last thirty years. Before that, I had a wonderful letterer. Abe Kanegson, who disappeared. He was incredible — an intelligent, literate guy. In the afternoons he used to play his guitar in the studio and we'd sit around and talk. [Jules] Feiffer was there; Feiffer was a good friend of his. Abe stuttered very badly, but when he worked, he could letter Old English lettering just the way you and I would letter anything else. Ultimately, I lettered all of *Contract with God* myself.

In *A Contract with God*, Eisner began to do all his own lettering.
© *1978 Will Eisner*

**MILLER:** That was really a departure.

**EISNER:** Oh, it was a big departure. I was a lot older. I had seen the elephant and talked to the owl *[Miller laughs]*! I was more mature, and I had something to say. I knew where I was going, I knew what I wanted to do, and fortunately I had a few coins in my pocket and was able to take the gamble. I was willing to face the fact that this thing could go nowhere and nobody would want it.

**MILLER:** A lot of us regard that as a turning point.

**EISNER:** I'm glad to hear that.

**MILLER:** You got to us. We started regarding ourselves as novelists. It's as if you said, "These'll be permanent."

**EISNER:** Well, I was trying, but I wasn't aware that I was making a revolution. I knew what I was doing was different because I *meant* it to be different, and I was talking to a totally different reader.

**MILLER:** Well, the reason it hit was also because we were familiar with the *Spirit* stuff that you'd done, so to have a new release out of you, and then for it to be a statement about format and intent, was a good one-two punch.

**EISNER:** Well, *The Spirit* was an easy thing, in the sense that I had no competition. No one told me what not to do. I was after a totally different reader. One of the reasons I took on *The Spirit* was really because they were offering me a new audience. It was a tremendous risk. The Eisner & Iger corporation was making money. I was making more money at Eisner & Iger than I had ever made in my life before that. As Iger put it to me, he said, "You're stupid to do this, because you're 21 years old and the war's coming on and you're going to be drafted. Who knows how long that thing's going to run in newspapers? If you're out, you're out, and you're going to be back to running around with a black portfolio when the war is over. If you survive." Nevertheless, I wanted to do it.

I sold Iger the company for buttons, really. Peanuts. He used to go around boasting about how cheap he got the company. And as far as I was concerned, *The Spirit* was a new adventure. All my life I've done things like that, I guess instinctively. I guess I'm like a guy with a mission who believes that what he's doing is right. I felt, not immortal, but I felt like a guy who is going into combat, believing the bullets won't hit him.

## "I wasn't aware that I was making a revolution."

**MILLER:** I think that has to be part of anybody's attitude starting any project, to tell the truth. If you don't feel that way, you'll have stage fright the whole time.

**EISNER:** Look, I don't know about you, but this book I'm working on [*Fagin the Jew*] is going to take me anywhere from six to eight months to do. I'm going to spend six to eight months of my life — that's a very precious thing to me now. It wasn't so precious when I was forty years old. I could afford to piss away a year. But now I can't afford to waste a whole year. If that book doesn't sell, I wind up with maybe ten dollars an hour for the time I worked on it. From a dollar point of view, it isn't worth it. There's got to be something bigger, something more to it.

**MILLER:** I haven't gotten back to this again, but for me it was a real breakthrough when I did one of the *Sin City* books [*Family Values*] as a single volume. It was 126 pages that I did in my studio, and nobody saw it until it was done. It was one of the most paranoid and exhilarating

In this scene from *The Dreamer*, Eisner's thinly disguised autobiographical tale, the artist recounts his reasons for dissolving the partnership with Jerry Iger.
© 1986 Will Eisner

experiences that I've ever had in the profession. Because I would occasionally become convinced that none of it made any sense.

**EISNER:** You go through that, yes.

**MILLER:** I didn't get any objective view of it hardly at all. I barely showed it to Lynn [Varley]. But it was five months of my life ripping through this book, and toward the end I was inking across twenty pages in a day. I was touching twenty pages in a day, and at the end of it, I felt like I'd run a marathon. So I send this steaming, smoking stack of pages in a Federal Express box to my editor, and it practically breaks the tiles in her floor! It's a wonderful feeling to do that much in a streak without chapter breaks, without issues — nothing. Just let the whole story take the shape it wants.

## "American comics are so constipated."

**EISNER:** But the whole point is that you're doing something for certain publication. *A Contract with God* was the first time in my career that I had no publisher. I had nothing presold. I didn't know who was going to buy this, or whether anybody would. And to this day, even though I have customers for my books, I don't know how well any particular book's going to do. Whether it'll be worth the investment. There's no one who tells you, "Hey, this is one of the great books of your life. This is a great idea; you're going to make a big change in this world." *You* gotta believe it. *Fagin the Jew* … I believe *it* might well make a difference. You have to believe in what you're doing. You have to believe in yourself, and you have to be willing to take the risk. That's if you're doing graphic novels and working on your own. If you're working for a publishing house, it's a different story. Then the question is: Is my work going to be really good this time around, when I show off my art?

***Sin City: Family Values*** was Miller's first direct-to-graphic-novel approach, which the author found both a "paranoid and exhilarating" experience.
© *1997 Frank Miller, Inc.*

**MILLER:** There it's always a mixed bag, because you'll have your own creative goal but you're clearly working within a set of restrictions you wouldn't otherwise have. It's been fun romping with the superheroes again, but I just didn't realize that the porcelain was so easily shattered. It does freak them out when you start having fun with this stuff — it's very strange.

**EISNER:** I haven't seen what you did. I'll be curious to see it. How many pages is the book?

**MILLER:** Hundreds. I need hundreds of pages. The pamphlet has made us think like wage slaves. We need room! I need lots of pages to tell a story. I like big pictures. The pace that I'm after is somewhere between American comics and manga.[1] Manga's too quick for me, but American comics are so constipated, so slow. There are too many word balloons and so many panels.

**EISNER:** I guess that's why the Japanese publisher wouldn't buy my stuff. He said, "Your work is too dense" *[laughter]*.

---

[1]Here, Miller is referring to *Batman: Holy Terror*, a project he conceived sometime after the events of 9/11.

# 5. . . . . .
# SEXY

*The next morning Eisner picks Miller up at the hotel and then drives to his studio, which is in an office building five minutes' drive from Eisner's home.  During the drive they discuss the fun they have on the job.*

**MILLER:**  What are some of the things you love most about cartooning?

**EISNER:**  To me, inking is sexy.

**MILLER:**  Inking is very sexy!

**EISNER:**  It's like downhill skiing.

**MILLER:**  Especially brush.

..........................................................................................................
Opposite: The infamous P'Gell. © *1947 Will Eisner*

**EISNER:**  I've always used a brush.

**MILLER:**  The brush is the most erotic tool you could work with.

**EISNER:**  You're so right!  There's nothing like inking with a sable brush.

**MILLER:**  It's like alchemy.  Mixing inks just to get the right texture and color.  Mixing various blacks with various blues.  It's probably the most physically fun part of it.

## "Inking is sexy."

**EISNER:**  I would say yeah.  And the second level of enjoyment is roughing with the side of a soft lead pencil and composing a scene.  Composing a scene is critical.  It's the reason that Jack Kirby thought he was a writer, because he was composing scenes from a story that was told to him.

## "The brush is the most erotic tool you could work with."

**MILLER:**  Another particular pleasure for me lately — in fact, it's so much fun it almost feels like a hobby — is that because I'm changing my style, I've been doing a lot more caricatures of real people.  Not famous people, but funny-looking people, curious-looking people.  When I do my roughs for them, I have to do several because I distort and distort and distort, so it really *does* become a caricature rather than a photorealistic style.  One of my favorites is George Will.  It's hilarious.  He's about three heads tall.  He's this little guy with a little bow tie — he's an idiot!

**Inking is sexy!  From _Sin City: Hell and Back_ #9.** © 2000 Frank Miller, Inc.

**EISNER:** All my characters are people I've known in one way or another. I spend a lot of time on casting my characters. That's a very, very important part of this thing. I think that's one of the problems: a lot of these young people working in the field don't have enough life experience to be able to develop the necessary insight.

**MILLER:** I don't know. As with writing, every era has something to offer in a storyteller's life. The sheer energy of your twenties — the enthusiasm. Some of the other things the younger cartoonists might not have, but the energy is what they bring to the table.

> "Technique is secondary.
> Technique comes as a result of
> *how* you do *what* you do."

**EISNER:** Right. You should always have stories to tell. Your whole life is built on stories to tell.

**MILLER:** One of the things that improves over time is your accuracy.

**EISNER:** That's right. It depends on what you're telling. If you have a story to tell, then you're dependent on the people who are acting it out. If you don't have a story to tell, then you're creating a visceral, or sensory, experience. Like some movies, you don't need to have a story to tell, so you concentrate purely on style and technique. But technique is secondary. Technique comes as a result of *how* you do *what* you do.

**MILLER:** I've been around long enough to see what types of influences get passed along, and I've come to realize that, up until recently, the field has been pretty incestuous. People were drawing the way the previous generation had drawn, but not as well. The kids who've been coming in recently don't give a damn how comics have *been* done. They're coming from a very vibrant, youthful culture. I think we're gonna get a lot stronger in terms of visual thinking.

**EISNER:** What are they bringing?

**MILLER:** I'm not even sure what it is yet.

**EISNER:** Do they know what they're bringing?

**MILLER:** Some of them. For some of them it's observation, for some of them it's just plain attitude. But it freshens up my eyes to see the work of somebody who, frankly, doesn't know he "shouldn't" do something, and to see how sometimes it works anyhow! It sharpens me up a lot. But mostly I just like to absorb the pure joy they bring to it.

Drawing is physical. I moved into my big New York studio. This has changed how I draw. I draw bigger. I draw my pictures standing up. Every inch of my studio is workspace, including the walls.

**EISNER:** I think that contributes to the feeling that you're involved in a serious enterprise.

# 6. · · · · ·

# INSIDE THE MASTER'S STUDIO

*The Eisner studio is behind an unassuming door among rows of lawyers', doctors', and dentists' offices. The studio is modest. Behind a glass door, there is a small reception area, with Will's posters lining the walls. A short hallway leads to Eisner's work area. On the left side is his business desk, which is surrounded by bookshelves and awards. To the right is his drawing area, where a drawing board, stacks of current pages, and a light table reside. Miller and Eisner take seats beside the drawing board.*

**MILLER:** How long has this lightbox been around?

**EISNER:** Since 1950, I guess. The carpenter came in and built it for us.

..........................................................................................

Opposite: Eisner's wash technique for *Fagin the Jew* involves using "dirty" water — i.e., the same water used to clean the ink brush. © *2003 Will Eisner*

**MILLER:** It's beautiful. Don't let [Charles] Brownstein see it; he'll try to steal it and auction it off for the Comic Book Legal Defense Fund *[laughs]*.

**EISNER:** I've got a lot of old stuff around here that I still use.

**MILLER:** I was lucky; I found the perfect drawing board. It must have been around 1985. It's an oak drawing board that has this built-in light table.

**EISNER:** Oooh!

**MILLER:** And since I do my roughs same size and lightbox them to pencil, it's a perfect drawing board. It's so well made that even though the movers tried to destroy it, they couldn't. I was able to get it fixed.

What kind of ink do you use?

**EISNER:** Higgins.

**MILLER:** Have you tried that new kind that Dr. Martin's puts out, the Hi-Carb?

**EISNER:** No, I use Black Magic.

**MILLER:** Black Magic, yeah, that's dark.

**EISNER:** Would you like to see some of the pages from the new book [*Fagin the Jew*]?

**MILLER:** Sure! Hmm *[appraising pages]*. A lot of wash in here.

**EISNER:** Yeah.

**MILLER:** I've never really messed with wash.

**EISNER:** I love it. The wash I'm using here is just dirty water. It's good to work with. And also it gives me a chance to deal with backgrounds a little more softly. Normally I ink every background in.

**MILLER:** This is beautiful. I'm loving the wash-work here. The depth of field you're getting … you're not drawing half the stuff back there, but I think it's *there.*

**EISNER:** That's exactly right. That's what I want. What I'm proud of is the fact that it's just dirty water *[laughs].* I wash my brush after two or three line strokes.

**MILLER:** Really?

**EISNER:** I keep wetting my brush and wiping it on a piece of paper. It keeps the carbon down.

**MILLER:** I may start doing that, because that's a problem I've got. I use so much black that you can imagine how often [carbon build-up] happens.

What's interesting is that here you're blurring your backgrounds but have included a few keys to indicate the environment of the scene. I was trained to draw entire rooms. That was the mark of a professional comics artist, that you would draw an entire office as your establishing shot and then come in for your close-ups. Over time, drawing entire rooms tended to be a rather boring thing to do — and it's pretty boring on the eye, unless you do it like Frank Lloyd Wright. I tend to love scenes more for their details than for the overall architecture of the situation. To me, the most memorable thing in your drawing area is the lamp on your board. That tells me more about the room than its dimensions. Often it's much better to find an object and build a scene around it.

**EISNER:** You can establish an entire scene by faking a Tiffany lamp on a table with a doily, and if you have nothing else in there, it'll tell you what kind of room it is, what era, what's happening in there. You know that in a scene like that it will have to be a lady, not a slob in a backwards baseball cap!

**MILLER:** Not unless he's breaking in *[laughter]*.

**EISNER:** What I'm talking about stems from a series of conclusions, a stagecraft that comes from the Depression era. During the Depression era, the WPA [federal Work Projects Administration] theaters that I used to go to didn't have enough money to do full sets. So what they'd do is establish a scene: take a lamppost, stick it in the center of the stage, and it became a street scene. Maybe a few steps to show the front of some building. From that I learned that it's possible with good lighting, with key details, to establish a scene. Not only that, but I also learned that memory is impressionistic, and so I began to make my work more impressionistic. In *The Building,* structures drawn by a standard comic book clone would have had every damn window with all the panes carefully structured. I didn't have to do that for my kind of reader.

**Eisner establishes scenes with a few key visual indicators, as opposed to detailed backgrounds.** *Photo by Charles Brownstein.*

As a matter of fact, the best compliment I had, an affirmation of what I'm talking about, came to me when I was in Holland. Some guy came over to me and said, "Mr. Eisner, I just got back from New York, and you know, it looks just like your books." I took that as a great, great compliment, because it was exactly what I was doing: I was doing the story impressionistically. No one knows how many steps there really are on a stoop outside of a house — I know there are thirteen, but most people don't — and it's not important. What's important to know is that they are there and that they have a railing on the side and that there's a *feeling*. All you need is a little bit of it.

It has to do with what I call impressionism. That is the one connecting similarity between what you and I do. We're both working impressionistically.

## "Memory is impressionistic."

**MILLER:** Especially in *Sin City*. For instance, I started *Sin City* a couple of years after moving to Los Angeles, and I was swept up with the romance of the city. I'd been out east all my life, and then I started *Sin City* — and I'm never gonna name where it is, because it's nowhere. The next time I do it, it'll probably be in New York.

Anyway, what is L.A.? Who cares about the Hollywood sign? L.A. is great old cars, gorgeous women, palm trees, and terra-cotta tiling, and that's about all there is. So I developed ways of inking terra-cotta tiles, silhouettes of palm trees blowing in the wind, and flying cars and good-looking women.

**EISNER:** What you are doing is what [Joseph Mallord William] Turner, the English impressionistic painter, did. He drew a harbor that looked exactly like a ship-filled harbor, and when you got real close to it, it was nothing but a lot of little strokes, and when you stepped away from it, it was all there. But what was happening was that you were putting a lot in there that he was inviting you to put in, but *you* were putting it in. You were participating. And this is what's led me into the business of eliminating backgrounds. I spent a lot of time teaching the use of panels and creating a whole theology on the function of panels, which I still abide by, but it doesn't mean that they need to be used exclusively or always. Same with balloons. I no longer use expressionist balloons. I use simple ovals just to keep the text in, because my characters no longer need the support of the erratic balloon. But the point is that they no longer need too much background beyond the fact that it *suggests* what's going on. The thing I was showing you there, that background was all that was needed for thirteen pages: one little panel that shows the scene, and the reader remembers the rest of it.

**Miller's own version of Los Angeles impressionism, from the first issue of *Sin City: A Dame to Kill For*. © 1993 Frank Miller, Inc.**

**MILLER:** One of the things that makes historical work so difficult is that all of a sudden you *need* a detail. What did they use for a soup ladle in 480 B.C.? Those details are absolutely critical, because if you get them wrong, not only will people notice, but the work will not be as good. But you can stylize like crazy.

> "L.A. is great old cars, gorgeous women, palm trees, and terra-cotta tiling, and that's about all there is."

**EISNER:** If your story is wedded to that … but if your story is not wedded to that — your *Sin City* stories are not wedded to that infinite detail. They're essentially impressionistic work. They're as impressionistic as impressionist paintings. Pure impressionism, in my opinion, is that car hurtling down the road and you don't see background, but you know what's going on and you supply all the rest of it. That's the essence of impressionistic art, and I believe that's very important.

**MILLER:** I think one of the things I find so strange about a lot of the people reading comic books is that they always counted panels. They always want to make sure they've got enough panels in the comic. Now they're counting lines. So if it only has three lines, the guy didn't work hard enough.

**EISNER:** Really?

**MILLER:** They call it detail, but it's not detail, it's density of line. There's some strange aesthetic that's developed with these very, very liney comic books. It goes against the traditions of the medium.

**EISNER:** The ones that I see that have finely detailed backgrounds — accurately drawn windows and doorknobs, buttons and nails — are all very accurate, and I think that's wonderful, but it seems to me that it impedes the speed of the story. It slows up the flow.

**MILLER:** I find, for instance, that technically [Katsuhiro Otomo's] *Akira* is an astonishing piece of work, but the sheer scale of the linework, the architectural detail … after a while it's like, "Am I reading a story or going to class?" There's just so much — and that can be some kind of *statement*, like in [Geof] Darrow's stuff. He's an absurdist. He makes the real world so bizarre, where your surroundings look strange to you. But when it starts being all this information, it tends to overwhelm and get in the way of the narrative.

**Eisner's impressionistic architecture, from *The Building*. © 1987 Will Eisner**

**EISNER:** Well, I think this brings us to the content of the story, the nature of the story. Japanese *manga* use very little background in order to enhance the speed at which the story is moving. They want thin stories that move at an incredibly fast speed.

> "The rate of speed of a story is an important thing, but it depends on the story you want to tell. To show an entire building in infinite detail is not storytelling, as far as I'm concerned."

**MILLER:** They really do strive for movies on paper — it resembles film almost to the point of being flipbooks sometimes.

**EISNER:** And what they do is they eschew background in many cases. The rate of speed of a story is an important thing, but it depends on the story you want to tell. To show an entire building in infinite detail is not storytelling, as far as I'm concerned.

# 7.......

# KINK AND FREEDOM

*Miller and Eisner walk over to Will's business desk. Frank stops to look at a copy of a print, featuring the Spirit spanking Ellen Dolan, that's hanging on the wall.*

**MILLER:** I've gotta say, that spanking cover is one of the kinkiest things you ever did.

**EISNER:** *[Laughs]* I know. I've got the original art in the house.

**MILLER:** Somehow I've gotta do a riff on that in *Sin City [Eisner laughs]*.

**EISNER:** That would be really appropriate in *Sin City*.

..................................................................................................

**Opposite: The Spirit "spanking cover"! © 1950 Will Eisner**

**Femme fatales take the Spirit and Inspector Dolan in hand!** *© 1949 Will Eisner*

**MILLER:** Although it might be the *guy* who'd be getting spanked *[laughter]*.

**EISNER:** Well, I wasn't into kinky stuff. Spanking.

**MILLER:** Actually, one of the funniest threads you ever did was the one where the Spirit is holding forth to Dolan on how to control women, and they don't know they're both being held in a woman's hand *[laughter]*.

**EISNER:** Those were good years for me. I had absolutely all the freedom in the world. I could do whatever I wanted, and all I was doing was trying to talk to adults.

**MILLER:** You must have worked like *lightning*.

**EISNER:** Oh, I was working hard. Most pages were done one-a-day.

**MILLER:** You had to work a bit quicker than that when you were doing a weekly.

 **EISNER:** Yeah. As a matter of fact, I had to do it for *two* sizes, because two of the clients were printing it tabloid size, so I had to work larger, on a 22x29[-inch] board. The line had to be strong enough and solid enough. Originally I started out using Japanese brushes. Lou Fine and I were the only two guys who could use them, because you have to have a strong hand and a good wrist, since the brush does not snap back — it just lies there. You must be able to control it.

MOLLY
MOLLY

SELENA
SELENA

ABE

GERTA

# 8.......

# STAGES AND CREATIVITY

**MILLER:**  How do you approach making a book, Will?  What are your stages?

**EISNER:**  In this particular book, *The Name of the Game,* I started off with the characters.  I made pencil roughs of the characters *[shows the roughs to Miller]*.

**MILLER:**  These are Xeroxes.

**EISNER:**  These are pencil roughs.

**MILLER:**  No, I mean the other side is Xeroxes.

..........................................................................................

**Opposite: Preliminary character designs for Eisner's *Family Matter*.**
*© 1998 Will Eisner*

**EISNER:** Yeah, the other side. I'm a Depression boy. I don't throw stuff away. I save old paper.

After the characters I made a timeline, because one of the problems with the story was that I was going over something like forty, fifty years, so I made a timeline for all the people. Then I created the main characters I was going to deal with. The story breakdown I have here somewhere. Just envision a laundry list of incidents. I knew how it was going to end. I always start from that.

**MILLER:** The way I've taken to doing stories lately, especially since *DK2* with its captive audience, is when looking at broad strokes, I just started using Post-it notes for scenes, and put them all on the wall and kept rearranging them until the structure worked. I've still got them up there, because every once in a while, when I was feeling lost in the middle of the story, I would just walk up to that wall and there's the whole picture.

> "I'm a Depression boy.
> I don't throw stuff away.
> I save old paper."

**EISNER:** That's essentially what I do here, except with a basic story like this, I start off with where I want each character to be at a given time. I make a list and I'll say the character is doing this here, and each one of those is a page. I use pages almost like panels. I think of them as panels, and in each panel something complete happens. Within that panel I make other panels. In this particular case, I've been staying to three tiers. I'll make changes in the dummy as I go, too — for example, here, I changed the whole balloon. My pencil roughs, as you can see, are chopped off. I'm doing what you do. You do it on the wall; I'm doing it here.

**MILLER:** Well, no, plotting is what I put on the wall.

**EISNER:** The plotting depends on the kind of story. A lot depends on the complexity of the story you're doing. If you're doing an adventure story where there's a lot of action going on, then it would be essential to do it that way.

## "You believe in letting the publisher know what you're doing?!"

**MILLER:** Well, if the cast is large in any story …

**EISNER:** *The Name of the Game* is a huge cast, and they were growing old as the story went on; that's why I needed the timeline. As far as the compositions here are concerned, again, this is all chopped up. Essentially I'm doing these dummies as a selling piece, too. They tell the publisher what he's going to get.

**MILLER:** So you believe in letting the publisher know what you're doing?!

**EISNER:** Sure.

**MILLER:** You can't trust publishers, Will, come on *[laughs]*! No, I'm kidding.

**EISNER:** It isn't a question of trust …

**MILLER:** No, as long as I don't have to give them control.

**EISNER:** Well, there's a point about trust. I don't trust telling a guy something that I'm going to do, because I don't trust him to imagine

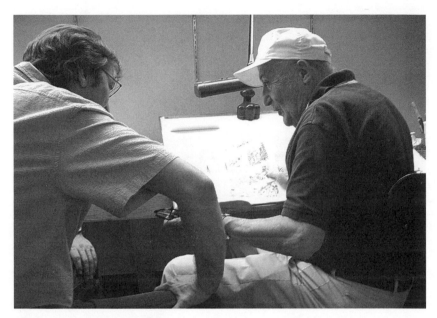

*Photo by Charles Brownstein.*

it exactly the way *I* would imagine it. If I say I'm going to have a guy jumping off a bridge and dying while he's in the water, the person I'm talking to has a vision of which side of the bridge the guy's going to jump off and how he's going to jump. I have a different vision. Over the years, I've always believed you don't sell by conversation, you sell by showing. You say to an editor, "This is what you're going to get. You want to buy it, or don't you want to buy it?" I no longer count on an editor understanding what it is I'm going to say. I don't believe in that. When you say I don't trust an editor ... is that what you mean?

**MILLER:** No, as a matter of fact, by the time I ever deliver much of anything, the editor's already so familiar with my story that they're probably sick of hearing about it! I talk incessantly. And when it comes to stuff where I don't own the properties, I deliver a very comprehensive scenario. But as far as the layouts and all of that ... for me, so much of that's done along the way, that I don't think I could deliver a facsimile of the entire thing at the start.

**EISNER:**  Remember, generally I'm used to dealing with five or six different publishers around the world, in different languages.  I give this [dummy copy] to my agent in Europe, and he sends it around to each of the clients and says, "This is what Will's going to do."  As far as they're concerned, this is already the new book.  One of them wanted to buy it as is!  When he came back and said that to me, I thought maybe I should add some wash to it and reset the balloons.  I don't think pencil roughs have the capacity of transmitting the kind of feeling of final art.

**MILLER:**  No, it would just be more of a document than the final product.

**EISNER:**  They tried to reproduce pencil art one time, you remember that?  Or maybe it was before you came in.  Somebody got the idea that: "What the hell do we need inkers for?  These guys can pencil so tight that we can reproduce them."  I think it was Stan Lee who tried that.

> **"I don't really regard the pencil as a drawing instrument.  It's very much like a stylus was during the Renaissance.  It's a structural tool.  Ink is a drawing medium."**

**MILLER:**  I think they've tried that six or seven times, and it never worked.

**EISNER:**  It never really works.  It doesn't make any sense, when you come right down to it.

**MILLER:**  I don't really regard the pencil as a drawing instrument.  It's very much like a stylus was during the Renaissance.  It's a structural tool.  Ink is a drawing medium.

**Eisner's pencil roughs, from the very last story he ever drew ...**

... and the finished version, in ink wash, as it was printed in *The Amazing Adventures of the Escapist #6.* ©2005 Will Eisner and Michael Chabon.

**EISNER:** I agree with you. And the problem is if the pencils are so tight, the inking becomes a mechanical thing. It loses the thing you and I were talking about, which is the joy of drawing.

**MILLER:** To me, it's absurd to hear about tight pencils, because you're adding a ridiculous step that means nothing.

**EISNER:** I don't do tight pencils. I compose or lay out a story. It's what I start with, so in the case of *The Name of the Game*, here, I'll start with this page. I position the balloons first. I ink the lettering and then the balloon around it. Within the space left by the balloons, I'll begin drawing. Balloons are subject to the composition.

I spend a lot of time on the postures, and the gestures, and the little details. I plan that.

The three stages that I use are: a rough pencil, and then maybe I'll tighten up with a mechanical pencil. Lou Fine used to use a mechanical

**Eisner begins to demonstrate the first stage of his drawing process: rough pencils.**
*Photo by Charles Brownstein.*

pencil; I learned how to use that from watching him . I'll lay out the shapes and a certain amount of detail. And then I ink. After I've done the linework, I'll put the wash in, my dirty-water wash. I'm so proud of that discovery!

I use a quill pen for the detail.

**MILLER:** I start with blue pencil. The thing I like about that is that it ultimately keeps the whole process cleaner.

**EISNER:** I originally used it for that reason. Because remember, when you're getting five or six dollars a page, if I'm only making $1.75 a page, I'd better cut out something. I finally began using preprinting panels.

Now I don't use the hole-punched plastic that you rule your lines with, for lettering. I use this … just a big piece of cardboard *[chuckles]*. I lay it on the board, use a triangle, and draw the line.

**MILLER:** No kidding! What I do is take the Ames lettering guide and letter it all in ink, and then lightbox the text onto the board. I write right on the board.

**EISNER:** Yeah, you've got a lightbox thing.

**MILLER:** I use a lightbox all the time.

**EISNER:** It's a very good thing. I don't use it, though. The reason I do the lettering that way is that I'm trying to sell this book to Europe and, here, to the uptown publishing houses, not the comic book houses. And [traditional lettering] feels too comic-booky.

**MILLER:** Let's get back to the whole method thing. My feeling is that it's almost a perfect straight line, with the job getting more fun at each stage. Plotting is a lot of work, with very little to show for it immediately.

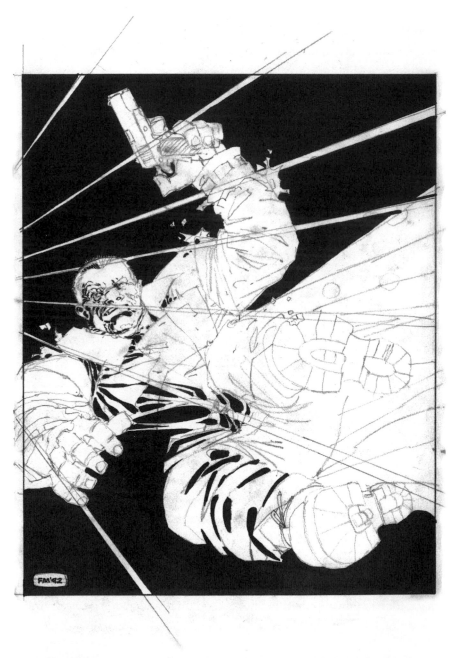

**Miller's idiosyncratic approach to inking: the artist lays in flat blacks through multiple-page chunks of a given story, if not through the entire story itself, before then going back and inking the detail work with a finer brush.  This page was completed in *Sin City: The Hard Goodbye*.  © *1992 Frank Miller, Inc.***

And as you're putting it together, the job is getting more and more focused and defining itself, and you get to know it.

**EISNER:** It's like musical composition. You try to come up with a melody — and suddenly it rises up, and once you hear the melody you can go.

**MILLER:** And then execution is a gas! When I did *Family Values,* that was my first nonstop single volume. Inking was the most amazing part of it because I had 126 pages to ink, which means I laid in the flat blacks across 126 pages and then I came in with a finer brush for the whole thing.

**EISNER:** I pencil and ink each page. You pencilled all the way and then inked all the way?

**MILLER:** Yeah. I laid it all out, then I pencilled all of it, then I lettered all of it, then I laid the flat blacks in across the whole thing.

**EISNER:** I can't do that because I lose my connection with the story.

**MILLER:** It depends on the stories you do, too. My stuff tends to want to go for momentum.

**EISNER:** Your stuff does move. Mine requires me to be involved with each page.

**MILLER:** I'm pretty involved; it's just a different kind of thing I'm after.

**EISNER:** It's a different involvement, but I'm curious to know about it because that's an unusual kind of thing. Traditionally, I've always worked — and the people who worked in my shop always worked — page by page.

**MILLER:** It's interesting the way it works for me, because it keeps me fresher. It keeps my eyes fresh at each stage. When I had those flat blacks laid down — because there's no line in it; it's just those flat areas of black — when I come to that page again, those flat blacks have dried and the page is brand new.  Also, I tend to be able to work simpler with less line, because I can see where it's needed and not.

**EISNER:**  Maybe I didn't understand.  You've got a 150-page book, you've laid it all out for 150 pages, and you do the text first?

**MILLER:**  I pencil it first.

**EISNER:**  You pencil the whole thing, all 150 pages in pencilled form, and then you go back and you start with page one again, doing the lettering all the way — that's the second step?

**MILLER:**  Yeah.

**EISNER:**  And then the third step is the inking of the art?

**MILLER:**  Yeah, but I do that in steps, too.  The way I do the inking is a little backwards, because I lay in the flat areas of black before I do any line.

**EISNER:**  So you're inking in two stages.

**MILLER:**  Yeah.  The best stage is the white-out.

**EISNER:**  Why?

**MILLER:**  Because it's fun!  I'm wiping it on my face.  It's like doing a war dance or something!  Also because, doing some of these stages, all of a sudden I'm producing so many finished pages it's idiotic.  Because I'll do the layouts in, like, ten in an hour, and it just rolls along.  I don't always do all 150 pages.  Sometimes I'll do a book in large chunks.  But I do work in many stages.

**EISNER:** Well, what you saw in the studio is the way I do it. I've always traditionally done it page by page by page, because each page is … like theater, it's a scene. A book is a series of scenes, like what I first was exposed to when I saw vaudeville as a kid: there were scenes that were called blackouts. Blackouts were little vignette scenes where the joke was told visually, and at the end of the joke all the lights went out. Like a nurse walks in and drops her pants, and then all the lights would go out. Those were called blackouts. So I work from scene to scene. Each page for me, the pages you were looking at in that story, each one is a sequence that has a beginning and an end. A lot of the comics I see today run along endlessly. They divide a movement of action between pages. I guess there's nothing wrong with it — it's another way of doing things — but it deals with a different rhythm of storytelling.

**MILLER:** That's interesting. Before I flew down to do this interview, someone said that your work moved more like theater and mine like film. I think it's reflected in the fact that I do put my books together like a film actor. As I'm working, I'll go, "I need something here." It'll feel like the timing needs a touch, so I'll add an image or even a page or even two pages. I like to keep it as fluid as possible.

**EISNER:** You're working more loosely. I'm working very tight. I may make a change in my scene. I'll spend some time moving the actors around. Maybe adding an extra scene, or instead of having a close-up, I'll have a long shot. But I do a page each day. You don't do what I do. I've gone through the stage of the long, sweeping thing. The rough dummy that you saw, that's where I did it.

**MILLER:** I end up with this ridiculous yard-thick stack of marker roughs on tracing paper! And often I'll do an image and then do the next panel on another sheet and then combine them with a pencil. So there are a lot of pieces to the way I work, and I'm very comfortable that way. Sometimes I just love leaving half a page blank — just because I can! Because I know that's gonna make the audience feel unsettled, since there's a disturbing piece of space.

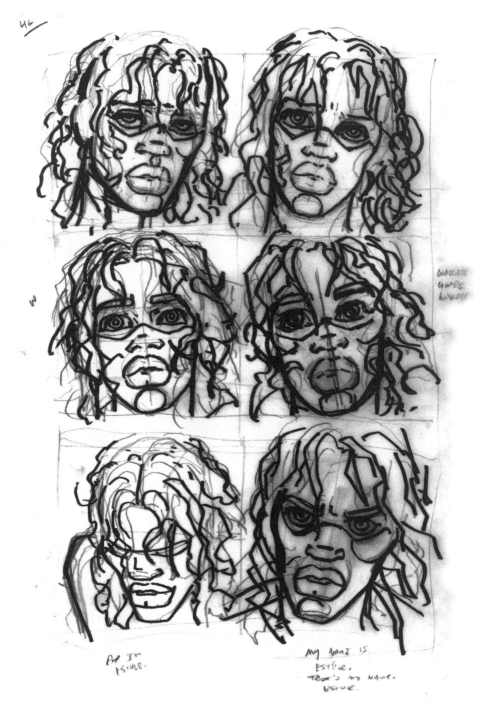

**A sample of Miller's "marker roughs" (printed in the _Sin City Sketchbook_) ...**

**... and the finished inks, from *Sin City: Hell and Back* #9.** ©*2000 Frank Miller, Inc.*

BOTH HOUSES OF CONGRESS RISE IN A STANDING OVATION FOR PRESIDENT RICKARD...
THANK YOU. THANK YOU. YOU'RE TOO KIND.
NOW, IT'S TAKEN SOME DOING--
YEAH, SOME DOING. LIKE REPEALING THE BILL OF RIGHTS!
OLSEN--WE HAVE SPONSORS TO THINK ABOUT.
--BUT WE HAVE ARRIVED. WE ARE AT PEACE--
YOU CAN'T STOP THINKING ABOUT IT...
AND YOU CAN HAVE IT...
OF COURSE WE'RE AT PEACE!
WE'VE KILLED JUST ABOUT EVERYBODY WHO DISAGREES WITH US!
--OUR CHILDREN LIVE IN A WORLD FREE OF CRIME--
OUR CHILDREN LIVE IN A DAMN POLICE STATE!
--WE ARE PROSPEROUS BEYOND THE DREAMS OF PREVIOUS GENERATIONS--
WE'RE WELL-PAID SLAVES!
WHO WILL STOP THIS?
YOU CAN HAVE IT. ANY TIME. DAY OR NIGHT...
MY PATIENCE IS AT ITS END.
THE TIME HAS COME.

# 9.· · · · · ·

# FILM, THEATER, AND FAMILY MATTERS

**MILLER:** I'd like to get into the idea that your work is more like theater and mine is more like film. I think I agree with the substance of that, although I do think the forms are very different. The whole reference to comics being movies on paper is a really corrupt one, because it makes us sound so inferior. *Manga* really do try to be movies on paper.

Off the top of my head, one of the things I like about film that works better in comics is the juxtaposition of contrasting or related images that are happening to take place at the same time. Because you do take in a page as an entity, and you're experiencing panel three when you're looking at panel one. Comics are static. We can imitate TV or the Internet, but we can't match them.

Opposite: Miller's work has long been described as highly cinematic, though certain movie-style tricks actually work better in the comics medium. This scene from the second volume of *DK2* illustrates comics' ability to juxtapose essentially simultaneous events within the context of one overriding frame: the page itself. © 2002 DC Comics, Inc.

To have the immediacy of all these overlapping heads chattering about what's going on and contradicting each other, to me, captures the onslaught of television.  I was trying to imitate channel surfing.

> ## "I'm in pursuit of a connection between me and the reader."

**EISNER:**  I have absolutely no intention of capturing the essence of any other medium.  I'm in pursuit of a connection between me and the reader.  The only other entertainment form that provides a real, live connection between the viewer and the actor is theater.  In live theater you are sitting there and watching a real thing happening.  On film, you're just a camera.  There's no sense of contact between you and the actors.  It's an experience that you immerse yourself in.  You're a spectator, and comics is a participatory form.

I want my reader to feel that he is watching something real.  I start everything I do with the words "believe me."  "Believe me," I say, "let me tell you this story."

Technically, I currently work from live theater because I no longer worry about getting bird's-eye views and special camera angles.  When people talked about the cinematic quality of *The Spirit*, that was because I realized when I was doing *The Spirit* that movies were creating a visual language and I had to use the same language, because when you are writing to an audience that is speaking Swahili, you'd better write in Swahili.  And that's what I was doing then.

**MILLER:**  Your focus is very much on the drama and the intimacy.  I enjoy evoking that kind of kinetic craziness that's the modern world.  I'm really fond of the relentless pace.  Some of the stories I've most enjoyed doing and am proudest of are fever dreams. Two hundred pages that take place in a single night, which is chaotic and frightening and weird and funny. I like that fast intensity.

I did *Family Values* that way. That was the first book I was able to put out in one chunk, the way you did with *A Contract with God*. In fact, it came out around the time *Family Matter* came out.

**EISNER:** I'm not sure I read *Family Values*. What was it?

**MILLER:** *Family Values* is a short story. It's not a novel. It's why I always love to use the word "yarn," because it's so unpretentious and it's kind of corny. But it also gives me the freedom to do whatever structure I want. It really was a story where I started with a punch line and worked my way backwards. I knew the theme was going to be a very sarcastic take on the term "family values" and the way that "family" is being thrown around like it's the *only* value we have these days.

**EISNER:** What was the story about?

> "I enjoy evoking that kind of kinetic craziness that's the modern world."

**MILLER:** Everybody in the book is part of a family, but I'm using "family" in different ways. So it's a study on the word *family*, but doing that as an adventure story.

I got mad, I got sick of hearing about family and values and children all the time, so I thought, "Yeah, let's take a look at what families *are*." So first you meet the mafia boss, and then a corrupt politician, and this alcoholic single mother character who's kind of pathetic but obviously concerned about her kid. Ultimately, the family that [the story] most counts for is a pair of lesbians, one of whom was killed accidentally during an assassination. And our hero has tracked it all down in order to bring in the other woman so she can wreak her vengeance on the mafia people.

And yet this is all done as a fever-pitched narrative.

**EISNER:** What devices did you use to reach that "fever pitch"?

**MILLER:** It was a conscious decision to do this as a book, without serializing it. And I decided I would come up with my story, simple as it was, and pace it any way I wanted. Let it breathe as much as it wanted and not think about page count. I had to break out of that pamphlet format.

Those were very intense months. I was doing layouts and then pencilling and inking, but then I would stop and go back and think, "This needs

**The four-page scene from *Family Values* where Dwight gets hit by a car ...**

to breathe more." There's one place where a man gets hit by a car, and it goes on for four pages before he hits the ground!  The book's structured to be a complete single unit.  There are no chapter breaks.

**EISNER:**  You mean the car hits the guy and he's flying around for four pages?  Almost like an opera where a guy is dying for three or four scenes?

**MILLER:**  It's not quite that extreme.  But the images are so large that when the car hits him, it's a double-page spread.

**EISNER:**  So you're using physical images rather than timing devices.

**MILLER:**  I'm finding that timing is becoming a concern that hits me pretty hard at each stage of the game, because I really am hung up on pacing.  I think that an advanced way to control the pace that isn't something clumsy — like a lot of text, or using repeated images as in film — is to charm the eye.  Or if you're really at the top of your game,

**... ouch, ouch, ouch — and "whuff"!** © *1997 Frank Miller, Inc.*

to confuse it just a little bit so that the reader is induced to linger.  So, in this case, I used many fewer words and much bolder images.

**EISNER:**  What does the reader linger on?  Is it a complex little image? Apparently this thing's moving along at the same rate of speed that *manga* do, it whips along …

Eisner prefers not to work with specialized camera angles any longer, opting for a less kinetic approach, akin to that of live theater.  **From *The Name of the Game*.**  © 2001 Will Eisner

**MILLER:** Very often it does, and then it slows and screeches to a halt.

**EISNER:** The problem with *manga* that I have is that while the story's moving along at a fast pace, there's no point at which I can stop and linger on it.

> "I think that an advanced way to control the pace that isn't something clumsy — like a lot of text, or using repeated images as in film — is to charm the eye."

**MILLER:** The obvious way to slow it down is simply for people to start talking. I had a very strange scene that I'm quite pleased with where our hero is getting the lowdown on what happened in the neighborhood from this alcoholic woman at the bar. The scene in the bar is very tense and sad and strange. And the story does torpedo along, but then there are moments like that.

When you ask what causes the reader to linger, the perfect example is [Bill Watterson's] *Calvin and Hobbes.* The drawings alone. You stop and look at them because they give you pleasure. The reader is charmed into lingering a bit. But it's not something I really believe in doing, in pacing a story.

**EISNER:** So, essentially, in *Family Values*, at the end of that book can I say that I know now what Frank Miller has to say about family?

**MILLER:** I think so. It's a pretty direct point.

**EISNER:** Because if that's what your mission was …

**The deadly assassin Miho easily despatches mafia-type hit men, as planned all along, in this humorous scene from *Family Values*.** *© 1997 Frank Miller, Inc.*

**MILLER:** All the respected figures and all the large establishments are based on family, and they're all thoroughly corrupt. And the only sympathetic figure is a single mother — again, not traditional family. And, again, the family that is revealed at the end of the story is made up of two lesbians and a tough guy who all come from a tough part of town full of hookers. *They're* the real family in the story.

I was a little sick of "mom and dad and the kids" being worshipped by everybody.

**EISNER:** I'm glad you're a little sick of it. Otherwise you wouldn't have done what you did. But, again, when I read a book, I'm looking for what it is this guy is telling me. After it's all over, it's the *way* he's telling it and *what* he's told me.  In between, the excitement that he may give me visually or the titillation that I might get from a very sexy scene is secondary to what I feel the main mission is.

**MILLER:**  Although I have to say that I think it's quite enough to simply be sarcastic about something.  I like to do that quite a lot, and it's one of my favorite things to look at.  That's why I think there's a thin line between melodrama and satire, and I like to dance across that line sometimes.  I like the story to take a very funny turn or have a character who is much more of a cartoon.

**EISNER:**  In that book, what was there that you regard as funny?

**MILLER:**  There's a running gag in it where our hero is hit by a car, and he flies through the air and lands, and these mafioso types come to pick him up because he's arranged for it.  They come in and pistol-whip him, and he's just admiring their car.  Earlier, the car he'd had to borrow was this horrible old Volkswagen that was barely running.  So he's this car freak who's saying, "I'm gonna love driving this thing," because he knows he's got his little assassin in there who's gonna take these guys out.  But all he talks about in that extended sequence is how much he loves that car and what a perfect model it is.  When the assassin starts attacking, he tells her not to hurt the upholstery.  And at the end of the book, after this gruesome ending, we just see him happily driving off in that car.

**EISNER:**  The mafia types didn't do anything to him?

**MILLER:**  Oh, no.  He had it all planned.  He was never in any danger because he had his own assassin waiting in the wings.

**EISNER:**  And the assassin killed the two guys?

**MILLER:**  Yeah.

**EISNER:** See, my *Family* [*Family Matter*] was dealing with a totally different question. Mine was written as a result of anger. I live in an area where there are a lot of old people who suddenly find that their families disintegrate on them. Ann [Eisner] is involved in this older-women's league, and she tells me stories about how their children do terrible things. This old woman was left some money by her husband, and her two kids continue to rob her of the money. And this is their *mother*! These stories that I do are usually built on truths that I feel need to be pointed out. I guess I'm being a reporter. Which is a little different than the other books being written in comics.

> **"Most of the plots being written in comics today are built on one very simple theme: pursuit and vengeance."**

Most of the plots being written in comics today are built on one very simple theme: pursuit and vengeance. That's the basic thing. "You killed my brother, now I'm going after you," and the whole book is about how he goes after the guy and ultimately kills him.

There was no vengeance in my story. The dynamics among family members was my theme. It was a very involved and very complex thing …

**MILLER:** You are saying that working within a certain mode, and working within a certain kind of story, is all about the same thing. So, in other words, a crime drama or a hyperactive story is always about the same thing. I think you're confusing form and content.

**EISNER:** Well, I guess crime dramas … are form … some have content.

**MILLER:** I stand by my genre!

**EISNER:** Well, I'm now taking a shot at the genre, I suppose, and maybe I shouldn't, because, really, I have no empirical evidence to support that, except that the comics that I see are all generally about pursuit and vengeance — with vengeance being the primary motive of the pursuit. Now, detective stories as a genre generally are a crime to unravel or an obvious mystery.

**MILLER:** I think they can be really, really painful.

**EISNER:** They may be painful in the process, yeah. A Sam Spade — or any Dashiell Hammett story — there's a lot of pain to it and a lot of agony. But it's still a pursuit story.

**MILLER:** In terms of plot it is, but in a novel like *The Maltese Falcon,* it's also a man's descent from self-contempt and his romance with a woman who he falls deeply in love with but then has to send down the river. And the novel's climax in particular is very different from the movie, because in the novel he was completely cold about it, and it was bad business that they parted on. Just because it would have affected his income, he sent her down the river. Or that's how I interpreted it. There's a lot more to it than pursuit and vengeance.

**EISNER:** Obviously in the interim between pursuit and vengeance is the brilliance of Dashiell Hammett. There were a lot of guys other than Dashiell Hammett writing the same stuff all the time, but there was only one Dashiell Hammett, and he was able to add a dimension to what he was doing. That's where the brilliance is. What I was doing was classifying or categorizing [in general].

A reviewer said my *Family Matter* had a Chekhov quality to it. He classified me with the Chekhov structure, which is a complex and involved kind of thing, and what I sat down to do, obviously, was a tapestry. I was working on a complex tapestry of involvements. Nobody was a villain. I didn't want anybody to be a villain or a hero.

**The mercy killing, from *A Family Matter*.** © *1998 Will Eisner*

**MILLER:** There was plenty of evil running around in *Family Matter*.

**EISNER:** Yes, there was evil in their involvement, but none of these people were doing things out of sheer evil intent. They were victims of their own lifestyle. The only hero was the little boy who was slightly demented, who mercy-kills his grandfather. And I did that very carefully ...

**MILLER:** It's a delicate piece of work. One of the things is that it's such an ensemble piece. The event that's happening is happening across a whole host of characters. The entire cast is a character. And it's a very self-destructive character; it becomes a host of emotions and decisions that are made, and there's evil and good running very subtle currents through it all. It struck me as one of those family get-togethers that big families tend to have and *something ugly's going down*. You can't put your finger on it, but everybody's part of a communal act.

**EISNER:** You bring up a very good point, because everybody who's experienced a family get-together feels somewhat the way you feel. I think a family get-together is a moment when real people are collected in a pocket of time. To answer your observation, what I was conscious of was that I was putting together a group of people who provided the scene so that I could do what I did at the end of the story: which is the business of a guy finally dying in the face of all these people trying to deal with it.

**MILLER:** It also has a group-mind that kicks in. There is a cult-like aspect to families.

**EISNER:** It's a tribal thing. Families are little tribes.

**MILLER:** And a function of tribes, for instance, is that they must pick their scapegoat — and often without reason, without logic. In this hidden Zeitgeist a scapegoat is chosen. What I found interesting here is that you read this whole book and never once wonder why these people haven't *left!* It was a really unpleasant place to be …

**EISNER:** They couldn't, because they were connected. The money was the connection; it was the wire that held all these people together. But there was another connection: the fact that they're *family*. There is a tribal instinct. I tried to articulate that at one point, where the wealthiest one of this group shows up because it's her *parent*. The woman who was taking care of the old man, she kept holding this family together because it *was* family. There is a tribal reason for it. The function of a tribe is to provide you with protection against the rest of the world. That's the real function of a family.

In *The Name of the Game* I pursue the whole business of family there, too. This upper-crust family felt that their family was a valuable asset. At one point a guy says to his brother, who is a drunkard, "You are ruining the family name." And [the drunkard] laughs and says, "Family name!" — deriding his brother's feeling of family.

**The family name as a valuable asset. From *The Name of the Game*.**
*© 2001 Will Eisner*

**MILLER:** The other thing is that family means different things to different people, in terms of intensity. There are people for whom family is the single value of their lives.

**EISNER:** That's because they're belonging to something. It gives them an identity. These very wealthy people, the Rockefeller family, have an "identity."

**MILLER:** There is some stuff running through the two books that I didn't realize, because both are ruminations and rather dark views. My *Family* book is more of the broadside and very sarcastic.

**EISNER:** Yours is physically violent, mine is emotionally violent. We both dealt in violence here.

**MILLER:** Thematically, too. You do feel trapped on these pages. There's so much medium-shot. You're always with several people; you're never by yourself. And you can't leave the room.

**EISNER:** It's stagecraft. I've been doing the old Charlie Chaplin perspective. The camera never moves. I wanted people to be involved in this thing the way that you're talking about. What you just articulated here is something very satisfying, because as you were talking you realized that's a universal thing, and this is what I'm looking for.

**MILLER:** The other thing I think the books both enjoy is that they both have the word "family" in their titles, and neither is a bromide. They're *not* reassuring pieces of work.

**EISNER:** Somebody looking at your book or looking at my book is going to say, "My family is like that," or "My family is not like that." Or somebody's going to say, "Yeah, that's *just* like my family."

**MILLER:** With a smile!

**EISNER:** With a smile because "I'm no longer a part of it! I've left it!" *[Laughter]*

# 10.......

# COLOR
# TECHNOLOGY

**MILLER:** One thing I want to start playing with once I've learned my way around the computer is to scan in some of my black-and-whites and come up with a variation on old duoshade. I'm sure it would be remarkably easy to do, and it would be absolutely accurate.

**EISNER:** I bought a Wacom tablet one time, I spent about four hundred bucks on it after [Scott] McCloud talked me into it, and I was unable to use it. Scanning a piece of art and then laying in colors like that, I don't know if you can do that on a computer as easily as you can do it with your own brush on a drawing board.

**MILLER:** No, I'm talking about just using a computer for the tones. The line art I'd do on board and scan it. It would be on a computer then, and then I'd use Photoshop to lay in the tone. Lynn [Varley] will probably be able to teach me how to do that in an afternoon, because she knows her way around the computer. It just seems to me to be a really clean way to capture what used to be done with Benday [dots], but I haven't seen good Benday in a long time.[1]

**EISNER:** In *The Name of the Game* I did the linework, and then I took a photocopy of the linework and with magic marker indicated where I wanted the Benday. They put it in with a computer, and it came out beautiful.

**MILLER:** That's the kind of thing I want to start playing with, because I've got a story that would lend itself to that Benday look quite a bit. It's a story set in the fifties, and for my generation the fifties happened in black-and-white. I think that it would, for one thing, get me used to using the tool, because it's something I do want to learn.

**EISNER:** Are you going to take the stylus and actually … ?

**MILLER:** Perhaps to lay in the tones, but not for the original drawings.

**EISNER:** I know — I mean, on the screen will you put in the tones with Photoshop?

**MILLER:** Photoshop is what's generally used. It's a program for retouching photographs that's been adapted to using artwork, so it has a very strange personality where whatever you do wants to turn into a photograph, to go smoother than you might want it. One of the things that Lynn's had to do is force it to be *wrong*. And there are places where she's come in and … what was it that [Bernie] Krigstein used? Was it zip-a-tone, where he got those grays, when he did smoke and such?

......................................................................................................

[1] Short for Benjamin Day, "Benday" refers to the dot-process of traditional color printing in comics. In black-and-white, these relatively large dots could presumably be made to emulate the look of duoshade.

**EISNER:** With zip-a-tone you won't ever get a soft edge.

**MILLER:** No — to make it look crude, like it's cut with an X-acto knife.

**EISNER:** It was zip-a-tone, then.

**MILLER:** Okay, it was zip. I used to use zip. It's nasty stuff; it takes forever.

**EISNER:** What I did on one of my books was put tracing film over it and then I painted spots.

**MILLER:** You basically did a rubylith on it.[2]

**EISNER:** It was not a rubylith; I would paint in the grays.

**MILLER:** There used to be an awful lot of sad-looking women who did that kind of color [separation] work all day long.

**EISNER:** Did you ever see those shops?

**MILLER:** I went to Chemical Color. DC had me and Lynn go over there as we were gearing up to do *Ronin*, and it was a rather stunning place. It was where the separations were made by hand, based on a colorist's color guides. Back then the colorists would work in Dr. Martin's dyes on photostats and Xeroxes of the artwork.

**EISNER:** And a code system.

**MILLER:** Yeah, which would all be coded to the proper percentages. The color guides were sent to this place that had a sweatshop feel to it, where they would dutifully hand-separate the pages. Do each layer,

.............................................................................................................................

[2] Rubylith is a red (or amber) acetate film used in the traditonal, hand-cut process of color separation.

THE BROODING OBSESSION THAT GRIPS YOUR MIND HAS YOU TOTTERING ON THE BRINK OF MADNESS, TOM GIBSON. YOUR TORTURED DREAMS ARE AN UNENDING REPETITION OF THE NAGGING THEME YOU'VE GONE THROUGH DURING THE DAY...

EVERY *NERVE* ... EVERY *PARTICLE* OF FLESH BURNED, MIKE...*SCORCHED!* YOU'LL EVEN SMELL YOUR-SELF BURNING, MIKE! HEAT, MIKE! BIG HEAT! YOU'LL *DIE,* MIKE...*BURNED ALIVE* BY THE LAW!

An example of Krigstein's signature use of zip-a-tone, from *Shock SuspenStories* #15. © *1954 EC Publications*

coloring it down, brushing all the red plates and the blue plates and the yellow plates.

**EISNER:** I only had two tones: I had solid-one and -two, one being twenty percent, two being fifty percent. The two tones only [resulted in] about thirty-five colors.

**MILLER:** Now it's in the thousands because it's digital.

The technology's really changed. My first work was published on letterpress, the paper they used to do newspapers on. It's the crudest possible printing: this is like a step beyond Gutenberg here! Then it switched to offset, which is a much more elegant process, and which they still use today. The first revolution was more of an aesthetic one, because the technology was there, but once we took the bait from the Europeans and decided to upgrade — have painted comics and so on — and to compete with them on a production level, the more the work became photo-separated.

**EISNER:** What you were talking about is what it was when I came in. The color separation was very interesting. The reason color separation was what it was: the unions charged 75 cents a square inch for half-tone and 25 cents a square inch for solid line engravings. The way they did color separation is that they would make four line-plates with zip-a-tone on each plate and angled so it wouldn't have a moiré. And each plate would print in a basic color, hence *four* color plates. And what we had were line-plates, so the publisher paid for four line-plates, not four *color* plates.

**MILLER:** The first time I worked with Lynn was on an issue of *Daredevil* [#191], and she colored it on acetate with Dr. Martin's dyes. The next book we did together was *Ronin*, which she did with gouache on bluelines.[3] And then we worked that way up until the new book [*DK2*] — except for *300*, which was painted on blacklines. *DK2* is the first thing she's done digitally. So it's amazing the number of tools I've seen her use, while mine have stayed pretty much the same.

**EISNER:** You had stages. I wasn't conscious of the fact that we were pushed into this by the Europeans. I think we pushed into this thing because of the availability of the technology. As offset came along, it was no longer necessary to do color by the hand-separations that we were talking about. They could do it photographically. Then when scanning came along, what they did was reduce pictures to numbers: ones and zeroes. So what they were able to do, then, was bring the scanning process into the business itself, and with the arrival of the scanning process you could then take an oil painting, or the gouache painting that your wife would make, and print it — and it probably would cost less than it did when they had to do it all by hand.

.................................................................................................................

[3] Bluelines (as well as graylines or blacklines) refer to specific painting processes used in comics coloring, wherein the colorist paints on a *print* — made with blue, gray, or black ink — of the original line art.

**MILLER:** What you're seeing here is a perfect example that comics has a history of following technology that wasn't built for it. Letterpress was designed to print type.

**EISNER:** And comic books weren't designed to be comic *books*! In those days the printing process was devoted to the comics section, but not a book. A book was the result of —

> **"Comics has a history of following technology that wasn't built for it."**

**MILLER:** And now we're coloring our comics on a photo-retouching program. We're scavengers. And we're always wearing the wrong pants to the party, too!

**EISNER:** You call it scavengers, I call it adapters. We *adapt*.

**MILLER:** It's interesting. When Lynn and I went to Chemical Color, it was a really depressing thing. I saw the reason I was told I wasn't allowed to do bleeds off the sides of the pages, and it was an undersized frame on the camera. It would've cost about a hundred bucks to replace, and that kept us from doing bleeds for decades.

**EISNER:** It would have cut into the profit margin.

**MILLER:** I would press the point. It's not the profit margin; it also had to do with the essential worthlessness of the product itself. There wasn't a sense that comics were a worthwhile thing, and that's a big part of the psychology that's had to change.

**EISNER:** That's an interesting point, because I never really dwell on it, but it has to be validated. [Our comics] weren't considered like an illustration for the *Saturday Evening Post*. For it, they'd spend the extra hundred dollars.

**MILLER:** How about all the comics with color bars across the top that they wouldn't even bother to strip?

**EISNER:** The original comics, printed on rotary web presses, had a difficult time getting registration. In fact, even the original front covers of the pulps were always done in three colors: blue, red, and yellow. No black. The red and blue were printed on top of each other to create a black. If you look at the early [Howard] Pyle paintings that were done for *Robinson Crusoe*, they were done with three colors of ink. And they were done on letterpress. Early printing presses had trouble with registration.

> **"There wasn't a sense that comics were a worthwhile thing, and that's a big part of the psychology that's had to change."**

**MILLER:** The limitations of the hand-done seps … the limited palette from that developed a pretty fascinating aesthetic that you can see in EC comics, and so on.

In a way, we may be coming full circle with the computer, because it offers up a chance to be arbitrary. Sure, you can make [the image] look like a photograph, and that's what everybody's doing, but there are all kinds of new ways to go with it. It's work in progress, I have to say. I haven't even gotten my fingers wet with the computer, so I don't know where that's gonna take things.

**EISNER:**  You consciously jumped from letterpress to full-color offset. What has that done to the content of what you do?

**MILLER:**  It works the other way.  The content determines whether or not I'm gonna do that.  Working with Lynn made me realize that I can tell any story I want to if I can draw it.

**EISNER:**  In other words, you can attempt a kind of depth of story.

**MILLER:**  Yeah.  I did a graphic novel with her that was an attempt at horror in full color [*Elektra Lives Again*].  It was not dark.  The entire thing was set in daylight, and the idea was just to get under people's skin in different ways with the color.  And I did it "clear-line."[4]

> ## "When I came back [into comics], the new technology was right there waiting for me."

**EISNER:**  You couldn't have done that back in the early 1970s?

**MILLER:**  We didn't have the palette; there's no way.

**EISNER:**  As far as I'm concerned, when I came back [into comics], the new technology was right there waiting for me; I could print in one-color brown.  I couldn't do that in the days of *The Spirit*.  I did a character in one of the *Spirit* stories that was a ghost, and I wanted him printed only in blue.  I got a call from the print shop and they said, "We can't do that." I said, "What do you mean you can't do that?  You're talking to a guy who worked in a print shop."  He says, "It's gotta be in black."  I said, "Well, drop it out of the black plate and leave it only in the blue plate; that's all

[4] The "clear-line" art style, best exemplified by Belgian cartoonist Hergé, is evidenced by equal line-weights, minimal texture, open spaces, and little to no shading.

you have to do." There was dead silence for a moment, then he said, "We can't do that." I said, "Well, why can't you do it?" And he said, "Because we never did it before." I said, "That's a good reason, huh? *Do it!*"

**"If ever there was a theme song for the business end of the industry, it's: 'We can't do that; we didn't do that yesterday.'"**

**MILLER:** *[Laughs]* If ever there was a theme song for the business end of the industry, it's: "We can't do that; we didn't do that yesterday."

**EISNER:** "We never did that before! No one ever does that! It's not done!" But that was something that was considered revolutionary at the time.

APPROVED BY THE COMICS CODE AUTHORITY

# 11.

# OLD-TIME CENSORS

**MILLER:** My only good color-hold story is part of my mischievous ongoing battle with the Comics Code back in the early eighties. I visited the offices — I knew a gal who worked there — I visited the offices and looked them over and realized that what the Comics Code [staff] looked at were black-and-white Xeroxes of the books. These were either approved or not; the changes were demanded [based] on *them*. They never saw the color, so I started printing blood all over my comics with red color holds, and they all got through the Comics Code *[laughter]*!

**EISNER:** I've never worked under the Comics Code. There are some funny stories about it.

**MILLER:** It's so stupid — all these rules that were written during the McCarthy era.

**Opposite: The Comics Code Authority's "stamp of approval." This particular design was in use circa the 1960s.**

**EISNER:** You know why [the publishers] did that: it was to prevent further governmental action on the industry. The movies did that and got away with it. So that's why publishers created the Code.

**MILLER:** The movie industry had the Hayes Office and then that awful ratings system. How was it for you to watch the Kefauver [Committee] Hearings happen?

**EISNER:** I was regarded as clean; that's why the Mike Wallace show invited me to speak, because I was doing a comic book in newspapers. Therefore, I was clean. I was not part of that "dirty, miserable crowd doing comic books." Because I was doing a comic book in newspapers, I was considered legitimate. That's why they invited me to debate this thing, to literally defend it. But the other comic book houses ... Bill Gaines [EC Comics publisher] was being humiliated at these hearings. He was trapped into a stupid defense. Sure, these comics had guys putting hypodermics in people's eyes — that was the kind of stuff that was selling on the stands — but nobody at the hearings ever picked up a clean comic book and said, "Hey, we also publish this. Are you going to let your kids read this, or *this*?" But nobody ever did that, and that's where comic book publishers got very defensive and got together and said, "We've gotta do something to prevent a government intervention." The whole thing was like a Soviet show trial. *Ugly!*

**MILLER:** Didn't they also just happen to write the Code sentence-by-sentence to shut down Bill Gaines?

**EISNER:** No.

**MILLER:** But they even prohibited the names of his books! Nothing with "crime" or "horror" in the title.

**EISNER:** I don't know. I wasn't present at the writing of this thing.

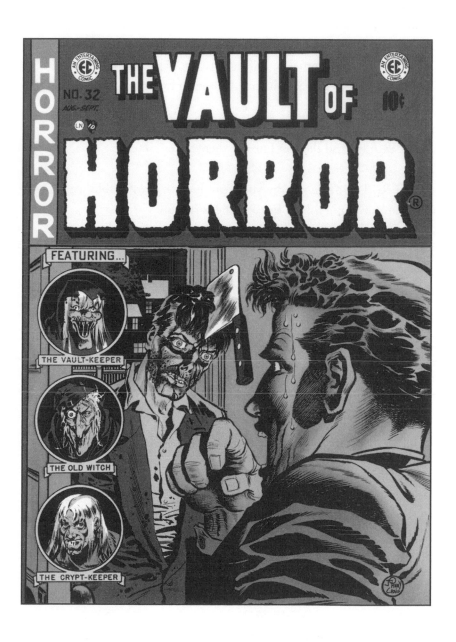

**A typically gruesome EC comic book cover, drawn by Johnny Craig.**
*© 1953 EC Publications*

**MILLER:** It seems to me it was a pretty shitty job, putting the best publisher out of business.

**EISNER:** Well, I don't know if he was the best publisher at the time. You call him the best publisher? I don't know if historians will agree with you.

**MILLER:** He had the best line out there at the time.

**EISNER:** I don't know why you'd call him the best publisher. Is that because he was publishing some of the best stuff … ?

**MILLER:** Because EC represented as high a quality standard as I've seen in commercial comics.

**EISNER:** Well, he had good people.

**MILLER:** Well, what else makes a good publisher?

**EISNER:** All right, I don't know.

**MILLER:** He published really good work.

**EISNER:** Oh, no, no — I just challenged why you selected him as the *best* publisher. Also, I don't know where you got your evidence for —

**MILLER:** I read the Code.

**EISNER:** But I don't think they sat down and designed it to put him out of business.

**MILLER:** It listed the titles of his books and said, "You can't use these titles, you can't use these genres!" Everything he did is listed there as being forbidden, and that's about *all* that's forbidden.

**EISNER:** They listed his books in the Code?

**MILLER:** They don't say, "No *Crime SuspenStories.*" They say, "There will be no comics with the word 'crime' in their title, or 'terror,' or 'horror.' There will be no living dead. There will be no stories that disrespect authority." It's pretty much a laundry list — that is, without outright saying, "There will be no EC comics," that's pretty much what it says.

**EISNER:** To me that's different. It's Charlie Biro[1] who was using the word "crime," so it was aimed at him, too, wasn't it? I challenge why you conclude that it was designed to put EC out of business; I'm not saying I know differently, I'm just challenging your assumption. I don't know whether it's true or not. I don't think it was written to put Gaines out of business.

**MILLER:** That's my understanding, at least.

**EISNER:** I think it was written to defend publishers against what they expected would be an avalanche of litigation that would put the comic book business *out* of business. The Carlino proposal, legislation in New York that I was debating against, was a law that Governor Dewey vetoed; it would have forbidden the sale of comic books on newsstands.

**MILLER:** You gotta love those old censors — they were so direct *[Eisner laughs]*. Nowadays they're so tricky about it.

**EISNER:** Historians dealing with a lot of facts made what I think are inaccurate conclusions. I suppose if you step back and look at it, from a historical perspective it was a time of shambles. Bill Gaines was thinking he was going to go out of business, and along comes Harvey Kurtzman who says to him, "I'll tell you what we can do: we can make a humor magazine. Give me a shot at this." And Gaines said, "Go ahead."

---

[1] Charles Biro was a writer and editor at Lev Gleason Publications, publishers of such successful forties and fifties comics as *Daredevil* and *Crime Does Not Pay*.

11. The letters of the word "crime" on a comics magazine cover shall never be appreciably greater in dimension than the other words contained in the title. The word "crime" shall never appear alone on a cover.

12. Restraint in the use of the word "crime" in titles or subtitles shall be exercised.

**General Standards — Part B**

1.  No comic magazine shall use the word horror or terror in its title. These words may be used judiciously in the body of the magazine. •

2.  All scenes of horror, excessive bloodshed, gory or gruesome crimes, depravity, lust, sadism, masochism shall not be permitted.

3.  All lurid, unsavory, gruesome illustrations shall be eliminated.

4.  Inclusion of stories dealing with evil shall be used or shall be published only where the intent is to illustrate a moral issue and in no case shall evil be presented alluringly nor so as to injure the sensibilities of the reader.

5.  Scenes dealing with, or instruments associated with walking dead, or torture shall not be used. Vampires, ghouls and werewolves shall be permitted to be used when handled in the classic tradition such as Frankenstein, Dracula and other high calibre literary works written by Edgar Allen Poe, Saki (H. H. Munro), Conan Doyle and other respected authors whose works are read in schools throughout the world.

6.  Narcotics or Drug addiction shall not be presented except as a vicious habit.

    Narcotics or Drug addiction or the illicit traffic in addiction-producing narcotics or drugs shall not be shown or described if the presentation:

    (a) Tends in any manner to encourage, stimulate or justify the use of such narcotics or drugs; or

    (b) Stresses, visually, by text or dialogue, their temporarily attractive effects; or

    (c) Suggests that the narcotics or drug habit may be quickly or easily broken; or

•   *The Board of Directors has ruled that a judicious use does not include the words "Horror" or "Terror" in story titles within the magazine.*

From the 1971 revised Comics Magazine Association of America Comics Code guidelines.

Harvey made *Mad* magazine, and it was done on newsprint in comic book form in the first issue, and it sold very well so they continued. Bill Gaines had been doing a Bible in comics form and offered to sell it to me because it wasn't selling with him. He said, "Would you be interested in buying this property from me?" This was Bill Gaines who, after his father died, took over his [father's] business after his mother ran the business for a short time. Harvey Kurtzman told me that Bill was a kind of ne'er-do-well, so his mother finally got him to go into the business and straighten out.

But nobody at the time really knew what they were doing, you're quite right about that. There was a certain amount of confusion, but no more confusion than there is in any popular business — the kind of business where they're selling hula-hoops and toys and games. It isn't the kind of central reasoning that you have, say, between Random House and Simon & Schuster or companies like that who regard themselves as responsible people and who are dealing with the culture of the time. There was a sense of dealing in drugs, I suppose — that comics were illegitimate merchandise.

## "I think there's something outlaw about the medium."

**MILLER:** It's interesting that there have been a few times that there's been an overall movement in comics, and it's always coincided with them getting in a little bit of trouble. Look at the fifties, and then look at the sixties when the undergrounds came out.[2] They were the cause of much

[2] Underground "comix," so called, grew out of the social unrest of the sixties. Printed in black-and-white, they challenged traditional mores and tended to feature both nudity and drug usage. Robert Crumb, Denis Kitchen, and Art Spiegelman are among the artists whose early work was published in the undergrounds.

**The public's ever-changing tastes during this "time of shambles."** From *The Spirit.* © *1950 Will Eisner*

consternation because they were vulgar, they were obscene, they were sold in head shops. In both cases, they were creative triumphs precisely because they were outrageous and daring, which is what I think comics are made to be. I think there's something outlaw about the medium that's gotta be who we are, and the worst thing we've ever done is sanitize ourselves.

**EISNER:** That's an interesting point, and I want to think about it. I have a sneaking, miserable suspicion that you might be right *[Miller laughs]*, and I'm trying to digest that and make sure I can find a reason to prove you wrong. That's an interesting conclusion to a series of facts that I think is worthy of talk.

**MILLER:** I think that's another one of those reasons why we had our own little British invasion — mostly of writers, but also of artists — in the eighties and nineties, when these cocky Brits came sauntering in, irreverent to the material, and really shook things up with stuff like *Judge Dredd* and then with the comics that eventually morphed into what [DC Comics imprint] Vertigo is. There was a sense of comics getting naughty again that I think turned a lot of people on. There was, of course, an immediate call for a ratings system!

> **"I have a sneaking, miserable suspicion that you might be right, and I'm trying to digest that and make sure I can find a reason to prove you wrong."**

**EISNER:** The whole period of the Kefauver Hearings was a shaking thing. There's no question about it. Working in comics at that time wasn't something your mother could tell her bridge ladies about. She was not proud of it. They put a stinking name on it; the whole thing was handled stupidly. Bill Gaines handled himself very weakly. Look, it was equally hard to fight McCarthy when he was riding high. Kefauver was a hard guy to fight.

**MILLER:** The curious thing about the hearings, though, is that so much was the result of that really insipid, badly written book by

Dr. [Fredric] Wertham [*Seduction of the Innocent*, 1954]. Have you read it? It really makes today's self-help books read like Freud in comparison. It's just trash!

**EISNER:** He made conclusions that weren't warranted. He was a psychiatrist, and he went around to juvenile delinquency halls, where they kept troubled kids in those days, and asked each kid, "What do you read? What do you do?" And every kid said he read comics! Ergo, it must be those comic books that are making these guys juvenile delinquents!

> *"Seduction of the Innocent really makes today's self-help books read like Freud in comparison. It's just trash!"*

**MILLER:** *[Laughs]* There's another brilliant leap of logic!

**EISNER:** He apologized for it later. Apparently he said that it was not exactly what he meant, that he was misunderstood. Candidly, I never did read the book.

**MILLER:** I've read it, and it's one of the shoddiest pieces of scholarship I've ever seen in my life.

**EISNER:** It did make an impact. It was a time when everybody was frightened. A Senate hearing at the time that was conducted … anything that threatens our children brings everybody out on the streets.

**MILLER:** Well, anytime anybody wants to stop anything, they say it threatens our *children*. That's just the button people press that always works.

**EISNER:** Of course it does. Unfortunately.

**MILLER:** I had an issue of *Hard Boiled* get in trouble, and the complaint was by a woman who found a copy of *Hard Boiled,* which has very graphic drawings by Geof Darrow, in her fourteen-year-old son's room and was convinced that was why her fourteen-year-old boy was moody. I was fourteen once. I didn't need *comic books* to be moody! There were strange chemical changes going on in my body that made me more moody than anything else *[laughter]*.

**EISNER:** Also, you were learning to hate your parents at that point, and you had good reason to do that: the bastards *understood* you! How the hell do you deal with a parent who understands you?

**MILLER:** Parents never understand their offspring. But it's an insipid thing that every generation *fears* its offspring. Imagine what the [Baby] Boomers are gonna go through when little spoiled Johnny turns fourteen and stops liking them.

> "I was fourteen once. I didn't need *comic books* to be moody! There were strange chemical changes going on in my body that made me more moody than anything else."

**EISNER:** Well, you have the drug business now. Look, that goes on and on, generation after generation. The same kind of thing happened in the 1800s, I'm sure, and the same thing's happening now.

**MILLER:** I think we're in for a big wave of it in about another eight to

**Miller and Darrow's *Hard Boiled* was cause for complaints against an Oshkosh, Wisconsin comics retailer in 1991.** *© 1991, 1992 Geof Darrow and Frank Miller, Inc.*

ten years. I think we're in for a major "What's turning our children into these large things that don't like us anymore?"

**EISNER:** I think that's the reason why parents are buying children's

**For his tireless efforts against censorship, Miller was awarded Defender of Liberty in 2002 by the Comic Book Legal Defense Fund.** *Photo by Diana Schutz.*

books in droves. The children's book market is the hottest market around, and it's because mother and father are both working and want to do something for little Johnny, so they buy him a five- or ten-dollar "children's book," which they both love. They think it's great stuff, they think it's very clever. What this means to me is that parents are reaching out to do something for their child; they're feeling guilty because they're neglecting him, because she's out working all day and he's out working all day and half the kids around are latchkey kids.

**MILLER:** To tell you how specious the arguments get that censors use, a couple of days after 9/11, I heard someone somehow blaming it on movie violence. Something tells me those al Qaeda guys were a pretty determined bunch and weren't swayed by any movies they saw.

# the AMAZING
# SPIDER-MAN

MARVEL COMICS GROUP 12¢

APPROVED BY THE COMICS CODE AUTHORITY

2 MAY

2 **GREAT NEW SPIDER-MAN THRILLERS!**

2 **GREAT NEW SUPER-VILLAINS!**

*featuring:* "The **VULTURE!**" *and...*

...SPIDER-MAN IS TRAPPED BY "the **TERRIBLE TINKERER!**"

DITKO

# 12.·····

# TALKING OUT
# OF SCHOOL

*Eisner and Miller break for the afternoon and go back to the house, where Ann Eisner has made a gourmet dinner. At the dinner table, beneath the gaze of African masks and of oil paintings Will created in his youth, the Eisners and Miller speak out of school.*

**EISNER:** Stan Lee showed a clear understanding and connection with his audience. He knew who the audience was and what it wanted. He had no pretenses of any intellectual demand in what he was doing. That was at the peak of Marvel's era.

The best proof of what I'm saying is that recently, when he started this Stan Lee Media thing, he created characters like the ones that he devised in the 1960s.

....................................................................................................

**Opposite: Steve Ditko's Spider-Man, with New York City in the background.**
*© 1963 Marvel Comics*

**MILLER:** When I was interviewed for TV recently, I was asked for my relationship to these characters and one of them was Spider-Man. I had to really be honest and say that *Spider-Man* would be known only as a fairly interesting comic book that came out in the sixties and had kind of a hipper tone to it, were it not for the rather blinding vision of Steve Ditko and the way he portrayed New York City. He gave that book all its romance. What Stan did was only one part of what happened.

**EISNER:** I'm delighted to see at long last that Ditko's getting credit for it. Do you realize that up until now Stan has never once mentioned Ditko?

**MILLER:** Stan wrote a piece in the *New York Times* crediting Ditko.

**EISNER:** Great! Anyway, go ahead, you were making a point.

## "Ditko gave *Spider-Man* all its romance."

**MILLER:** I was just saying that people so often attribute so much about what happened with Marvel Comics to Stan Lee, because writers are often the ones who talk history the best. People who draw for a living tend to have less free time, because drawing takes a long time, and artists tend to be less articulate. Jack [Kirby] was never as exposed as Stan Lee was. And Steve Ditko, he doesn't talk.

**ANN EISNER:** Is he alive?

**EISNER:** He's very reclusive.

**ANN EISNER:** Does he have a family?

**EISNER:** He has a son. I remember a long time ago, doing [the original interviews for] *Shop Talk*, I called Ditko up. Boy! It was like speaking to a Russian commissar! I couldn't get anywhere with him.

**Frank Miller's Spider-Man, with his version of New York City in the background.**
*© 1981 Marvel Comics*

FOOLS WILL TELL YOU THAT THERE CAN BE NO HONEST PERSON! THAT THERE ARE NO *BLACKS* OR *WHITES*..... THAT EVERYONE IS *GRAY!* BUT IF THERE ARE NO BLACKS OR WHITES, THERE CANNOT EVEN BE A *GRAY*... SINCE GRAYNESS IS JUST A MIXTURE OF BLACK AND WHITE! SO WHEN ONE KNOWS WHAT IS BLACK, *EVIL*, AND WHAT IS WHITE, *GOOD*, THERE CAN BE NO JUSTIFICA- TION FOR CHOOSING ANY PART OF *EVIL!* THOSE WHO DO SO CHOOSE, ARE NOT *GRAY* BUT *BLACK* AND *EVIL* ...AND THEY WILL BE TREATED ACCORDINGLY!

**Ditko's black-and-white moral arbiter, Mr. A.** © *1967 Steve Ditko*

**MILLER:** I talked to him once. He came up with a character in the early seventies called Mr. A that was clearly a reaction to what Ayn Rand was writing while the college kids were off debating the Vietnam War. It is the most morally arch character ever to be created. I grew up reading [Mr. A], and I thought it was one of the most amazing things ever written, because the diction in that stuff was so intense. He's this complete moral arbiter who just kills people if they're evil.

I got this notion in my head that I wanted to do an interpretation of the character, so I called Ditko up and said, "I'd like to do this as a team. We can tell the story however you want it. You can plot it, I'll plot it, whatever. I want to write the script, because I don't want the character to be as preachy, and I can get anybody I want to publish this thing because it's Ditko." And he said, "Mr. A's time has passed."

I said, "No, I can really make this happen. In fact, I want it to be in color. That's the whole thing — it's a black-and-white book, but the whole thing would be this black-and-white character in a color world. He'd be made out of marble, and with computer coloring, they can do texture that'll blow your mind." And he just couldn't handle the whole idea. Then he became convinced nobody would publish it. I could get *anybody* to publish that!

That's Ditko. But about Stan, how did you see the transition for Stan between working at Goodman's shop in the forties and then becoming the carnival huckster in the sixties?

Stan Lee began his comics career as an office boy at Timely/Atlas, a company owned by Lee's uncle, Martin Goodman, and the precursor to Marvel. From *Amazing Spider-Man* #7 by Stan Lee and Steve Ditko. © 1963 Marvel Comics

**EISNER:** He started out as an office boy in his uncle Martin Goodman's company. The comic book business was never organized. Most publishers would say to an editor, "Get us some good comics." An editor, to most publishers then, was a guy who corrected punctuation. Later on he was able to be the buyer …

**MILLER:** They turned back into that *[laughs]*.

**EISNER:** Years ago, Stan told me that his dream was to be in Hollywood, involved in movies. Early in his career I think he found doing this kind of promotional thing a good game, just as I found business a game and enjoyed it. His writing is really promotional. I don't mean that negatively — I think he would agree. His characters are usually pure circus. He would get someone like Jack Kirby, who was very receptive, and say, "Let me tell you a story." He'd tell Jack Kirby a story, and Jack would go away and come back with a completely penciled page based on the story as he understood it. Stan would then put in the dialogue balloons.

**MILLER:**  Was there even a story before Jack started pencilling it?

**EISNER:**  Well, it's as if I said to you, "Let me tell you a story about a guy who climbs Mount Everest and discovers a god up there."  Jack was a very structured guy.  It's only later that he began to feel he was somehow screwed out of what he should have had.  He thought he was a writer.  He wasn't really as much of a writer as Stan was a writer. And Stan thought he was a creator, and he wasn't really that much of a creator. I doubt whether he had to describe much to Ditko.  Stan was part of the separation of writer and artist in the evolution of comics.

Stan's a very interesting subject and, as a matter of fact, right now he's more interesting than he's ever been in his whole career.  Stan understood something that most people in this business never really understand.  He understood his market between 1960 and 1970 more than the average publisher in this business does today.  I have a great admiration for publishers who have that kind of visceral understanding.

**MILLER:**  Todd McFarlane [Image Comics publisher and creator of *Spawn*] has that visceral connection to the reader.

**EISNER:** He does.  He's writing to his own people.

> "Jack Kirby thought he was a writer.  He wasn't really as much of a writer as Stan Lee was a writer.  And Stan thought he was a creator, and he wasn't really that much of a creator."

**MILLER:**  The best way I've been able to describe it is: there's a moment when you're fourteen years old and you take your penknife out and you carve a swastika on your desk at school — Todd McFarlane *owns* that mind!

**ANN EISNER:** God, what a description *[the Eisners laugh]*! But even I can see that.

**EISNER:** Frank is never wishy-washy about his descriptions! Getting back to the point, Stan is a fascinating, fascinating guy. Ann complains because whenever I get together with Stan —

> **"There's a moment when you're fourteen years old and you take your penknife out and you carve a swastika on your desk at school — Todd McFarlane *owns* that mind!"**

**ANN EISNER:** Ugh, I cringe. They compete! Like two comedians.

**MILLER:** Him and Stan?

**ANN EISNER:** Yes, they compete! Verbally.

**MILLER:** Do what I do with [writer] Neil Gaiman. Say, "What do you draw?" *[Eisner laughs.]*

**EISNER:** I didn't know that you and Neil …

**MILLER:** No, Neil and I are great — we're buddies, but that's where I tease him.

**EISNER:** I did appear on stage with Stan a couple of years ago …

**ANN EISNER:** What I liked the best was when we had breakfast together and Stan suddenly got very confidential, and his wife was there, who seems like a very nice lady.

**EISNER:** She seemed at the same intellectual level as he.

**ANN EISNER:** She's an attractive woman. But Stan said, "All I ever really wanted to do was make money."

**EISNER:** Don't underestimate Stan.

> **"Jerry Robinson livened an Eisner Awards ceremony when he proposed a new award named after Bill Finger that would be for uncredited writers and artists and would be called 'The Finger,' and then he flashed his middle finger at the crowd!"**

**MILLER:** What about Bob Kane?

**ANN EISNER:** Oh, *Bob Kane.*

**EISNER:** Bob Kane. Bob Kane's a story.

**MILLER:** I had one encounter with Bob Kane that was so strange. I had just done *Dark Knight* [*Returns*], and he said, "What's with that? Why's that woman got swastikas all over?"

**ANN EISNER:** Let me just interrupt one second. I know that Will and Bob went to school together, so they're the same age. I think Bob was a little older than Will, a year or something.

**EISNER:** A couple of months.

**ANN EISNER:** Well, whatever. And I kept reading publicity about Bob Kane's age. It was getting younger and younger *[laughter]*. And I said, "Will, you're getting younger!"

**MILLER:** Actually, Will was known in his class as the one who *didn't* change his name.

**EISNER:** I didn't know what to change it to *[laughter]*. Bob was the luckiest man in the world you ever knew. He's an example of how to succeed out of pure luck.

**MILLER:** Did you ever read the story that Archie Goodwin wrote that was a parody of Bob Kane's career?

**EISNER:** No, he did a parody?

**MILLER:** It was about a guy who said he was an artist and hired a writer and then hired an artist, so he created a combo, but *he* wasn't there!

**EISNER:** I was on the phone the other day with Jerry Robinson, who was kind of sad about the whole thing.

**MILLER:** Oh, yeah, I've talked with Robinson. Robinson livened an Eisner Awards ceremony when he proposed a new award named after Bill Finger that would be for uncredited writers and artists and would be called "The Finger," and then he flashed his middle finger at the crowd *[laughter]*!

**EISNER:** The big thing I recall about Jerry Robinson is that he once said to Bob, "Look, you're very successful now, and you can afford to give me credit for what I did," and Bob said, "I don't see it that way." That was the end of that conversation.

**MILLER:** Geez.

**EISNER:**   Bob is a long story, but to go back to Stan, he should be respected for what he is …

**MILLER:** He's really hard not to like.

**EISNER:** I guess he likes me in his own way.  There's a genius in this man that's incredible.  He came along at a time when this business was purely a circus.  As a matter of fact, the reason Spider-Man is so successful and the other characters that remained the big hits are so successful is they're all circus.  Spider-Man is pure circus.

**The business of comics was a *circus* in the sixties, according to Eisner.
From *Fantastic Four* #3, by Stan Lee and Jack Kirby. © *1962 Marvel Comics***

**MILLER:** And they all had their circus adventures, quite literally.

**EISNER:** They all dressed like circus. Superman wore a circus costume. In the old days, when I went to the circus as a kid, all the strongmen wore exactly what Superman wears.

> "Bob Kane thought he was Frank Sinatra. We used to double-date, and I have stories about *that.*"

**MILLER:** See, I really think the reason why Superman and the rest all have the emblems on their chest is because the printing was so crappy that they had to put those names on the characters to tell who they were.

**EISNER:** The tights, the spandex, and the cape were straight out of the Barnum & Bailey Circus. Strongmen always wore capes, tight-fitting costumes. That was the symbolism. These were the iconographs that they chose. The reason their films are so successful is that they're circus: guys walking on high wires, flying through the air, flexing muscles. *Superman* did that, *Batman* does that, it's the same kind of thing. Bob Kane's first drawings of Batman came from the old silent movie serials.

**MILLER:** You don't think he ran around in a cape?

**EISNER:** No, Bob thought he was Frank Sinatra *[Miller laughs].* We used to double-date, and I have stories about *that [laughs].*

**ANN EISNER:** Be careful, you're being recorded.

**EISNER:** Oh, geez, yeah. I didn't realize. Hey, Stan, I'm only kidding! Don't get mad at me, Stan *[laughs]*!

**MILLER:** You haven't said anything damaging. I think he'd agree with every word you said, that he's a barker.

**EISNER:** What's happening now is he's lucked into this … I don't know how much he's gotten out of it, but in the last meeting I had with him, he said, "All I want to do is be rich. Will, what is rich?" And I said, "I don't know — depends on the way your neighbors live."

**MILLER:** Was he in a bad mood?

**EISNER:** No. He wanted to make money.

**MILLER:** He *is* rich. When was this conversation?

**EISNER:** Oh, four years ago. This was before his connection with the dot-com group. [1]

**MILLER:** Yeah, he's had a number of reversals since. He had that awful thing he did with DC Comics that tanked [*Just Imagine Stan Lee Creating the DC Universe*].

**EISNER:** I don't know what happened with that.

**MILLER:** It did really badly. It's terrible. It's still going, but everybody's moving the other way at this point.

**EISNER:** DC must have taken an awful shellacking. They must have paid a lot of money for what he did.

**MILLER:** They wanted me to be involved.

**EISNER:** What did they want to do? Re-create a whole new world?

[1] Eisner is referring to Stan Lee Media, whose co-founder, Peter Paul, was convicted in federal court on charges of stock manipulation, leading to the online company's crash.

**Stan Lee sandwiched between Will Eisner and Denis Kitchen, at the annual comics convention in San Diego, 1998.** *Photo courtesy of Denis Kitchen.*

**MILLER:** I think what they wanted to do was rub Marvel's face in it, to show that they could get Stan Lee as a headline name on a bunch of DC comics. And Stan got to have his name on a bunch of DC comics, but apparently it was a loser.

But you've known Stan since the thirties, so how has he evolved over that time?

**EISNER:** He hasn't evolved! *[Miller laughs.]* Everybody started as a clerk. *[Eisner points at Miller.]* You've evolved. The only reason I'm spending time with you is because no matter what I say and how insulting I am, still I regard you as an involving, growing person. But Stan has been Stan Lee ever since I knew him.

Here is a man who brought comics into Carnegie Hall. Did you know that?

**MILLER:** I didn't know that.

**EISNER:** He's the ultimate showman.

**MILLER:** We could use that right now, somebody who really has that kind of charisma.

**EISNER:** Well, I don't know. Something's happening now that I think doesn't need Stan Lee anymore. I think we need to promote content. I think comics is no longer a novelty.

> **"People are buying your stuff because it's Frank Miller, not because it's comics. They're buying me because it's me, not because it's comics."**

**MILLER:** Right.

**EISNER:** The medium's no longer a novelty.

**MILLER:** We have been assimilated, yeah.

**EISNER:** People are buying your stuff because it's Frank Miller, not because it's comics. They're buying me because it's me, not because it's comics. So we don't need anybody to promote comics as a thing — it's here. Stan had the incredible capacity to promote the medium, promote himself, and promote the characters. Stan hasn't changed. He has remained what he was and [that's] what he is today. What you're seeing today is what he was. He loves being involved in movies and theater and Hollywood. Hollywood is what he loves. At one point, he told me Marvel wasn't doing very well, and he said, "I want to be a television writer."

I have to tell you, about 1972 or '73 I had just sold my company, and he called me and said, "Will, I hear you're out of work." I said, "I've been out of work for years." He laughed and said, "Okay. Look, would you like to have lunch with me? I have something to talk with you about." So I said okay and came down. We had lunch and went to his office, and he was sitting at his desk and he said, "Look, I'd like to get to Hollywood. I want to get out of here. And the only way I can get out of here is to replace myself with somebody who has the business experience and has the respect of everybody in the industry." Then he called in his boss … I forget his name. He came from the book field.

**MILLER:** Oh, God. "The gulag is yours!" *[Laughs]* "Here are the keys to the gulag."

**EISNER:** His boss said to me, "Mr. Eisner, what would you do if you took Stan's place?" I said the first thing I'd do is create a royalty system. His eyes glazed over, he looked at Stan, Stan looked at him, and Stan shrugged as if the guy had said, "Where did you find this guy?" I said, "There's no reason why there shouldn't be a royalty. Actually, you have it in the book business." Anyway, it lasted about five minutes, I shook hands with him, he left. Stan said, "What do you think?" And I said, "Stan, this is a suicide mission. Try somebody else."

# 13.....

# AWARDS

*After dinner, Eisner and Miller retire to Will's library, which is decorated with original paintings and limited editions Will created over the decades.*

**MILLER:** How often do you get the pitch: "Let's use your name"?

**EISNER:** Quite a bit, and I'm very chintzy with it. In San Diego there's a contract between [the convention organizers and myself] that says I will recall the use of my name if there's any question in the matter of how they're running the awards or if there's any question of their veracity.

My relationship to the Eisner Awards is carefully separate. I have nothing to do with [the running of] it, and all I ask is that they don't violate the integrity of it. I think they are the best awards around. They canvass enough of the field so that everybody gets a shot, and those are the ones that I believe deserve it. I think the industry needs it.

..............................................................................................................

**Opposite: Will Eisner at the 1993 award ceremony that bears his name, held annually in San Diego, California.** *Photo courtesy of Comic-Con International.*

One year they brought up this big throne and set it down and made me sit on it. I felt silly … like an aged Vanna White standing there *[laughter]*. It was a loving gesture. I think now the Award has become important because a lot of guys are getting recognition for their work beyond publication, which they never would have gotten before. Creators can now say, "I'm an Eisner Award winner." It gives them status, and that's important. Same thing with the Harvey Awards.[1]

**MILLER:** Without question.

## "My relationship to the Eisner Awards is carefully separate."

**EISNER:** This is part of the growth of this medium. You see, you now have standards that are being set up — guys that are acknowledged by the rest of the community as being the best, for reasons other than just good sales.

**MILLER:** It must be a strange thing having an award named after you.

**EISNER:** It is, as a matter of fact. I want to tell you, Denis [Kitchen, Eisner's agent and former publisher] called me the other day and said [the Eisner Award committee] had nominated *The Name of the Game*, and I prayed, "Please, God, don't let them give me another award." What'll I say *[laughs]*?[2]

**MILLER:** Another Eisner for Eisner!

[1] Named after Harvey Kurtzman, creator of *Mad* and co-creator of *Little Annie Fanny*, among many others.

[2] In fact, Eisner did win the Eisner Award in 2002 for *The Name of the Game*, in the category of Best Graphic Album – New.

**The official Eisner Award logo.**

**EISNER:** What can I say *[laughs]*?

**MILLER:** You're both a presenter and a recipient.

**EISNER:** How can I answer Burne Hogarth, who said, "Will Eisner created that award so he could give himself awards"?

**MILLER:** Hogarth was a crabby guy anyway. You get cachet from awards, though.

**EISNER:** Very good, you get cachet. The function of an awards system should be — and in the comics business, so far, it has continued to be — an effort to establish or increase the standards of the medium. Remember that, as a young cartoonist, you're all eager to know what is

**Frank Miller at the 1996 Eisner Awards after winning in the Best Limited Series category for *Sin City: The Big Fat Kill*.** *Photo courtesy of Comic-Con International.*

regarded as *good* in the business, because you're aiming at that in your own work. Along comes a comic book guy whom we've never heard of who suddenly gets an Eisner Award. You look at his work as a young student and say, "Wow, if that is what is regarded by the professionals as being good, let me look at this again and see what *I* can do."

## "Burne Hogarth was a crabby guy."

**MILLER:** And part of the intimacy of our field … it is small enough that simple word of mouth accomplishes wonders. An award accomplishes a lot. At the same time, I've been surprised at the times I've simply briefly mentioned somebody's stuff in an interview and how that's had a ripple effect. It's changed their status a bit because they got mentioned by somebody who was established. I think the award system is a healthy part of that.

**EISNER:** I agree.

# 14.......

# BLOCKBUSTERS

**MILLER:** I think comic books are too obsessed with the same blockbuster mentality that makes bad movies. Every year there tends to be a big, sweeping, humongous project that seems to get the focus at the awards, and it makes me feel like people haven't seen much else of what's out that year.

**EISNER:** Frank, I don't think it's fair to say comic books are obsessed with something. I think the individual people involved with the field have targets. One of the targets is to produce a comic that ultimately will make a movie. Is that what you call the blockbuster mentality?

**MILLER:** That's not exactly what I mean. I think there's a comic book-type blockbuster that doesn't have anything to do with Hollywood. DC, in particular, seems to arrange a big, highly produced CPR job on their characters every year or so, and Marvel's been attempting to do the same thing. It's an attempt to create the thing that knocks everything else off the stands.

**EISNER:** Who is coming up with it — the editors, the publishers, or the cartoonists themselves? Very few guys are in total control. They're either pencillers, or inkers, or writers. Now, [Neil] Gaiman claims he's in control because he selects the artists who are going to work on his books. But he doesn't draw. But before we attempt to pursue that, who are we talking about? Are we talking about the publisher? Yeah, every publisher is looking for a blockbuster.

> **"This direct market is a very strange and almost paranoid fantasy that publishers are in. They're not embracing the fact that we're part of a wider publishing and entertainment business, and making full use of it."**

**MILLER:** Yeah, but I'm talking about everybody. The artist wants one, the writer wants one, the editor wants one, the publisher wants one, the retailers want one. I don't think it's a conspiracy.

**EISNER:** But who is in control of getting one? Is it the publisher who sits down with the editor? Is it a guy like [DC editor Mike] Carlin, who turns to the publisher and says, "Let's kill Superman; let's break this whole business apart"? And the publisher says, "Yeah, let's go with that." My impression of the function of editors today is that they're like buyers in a department store. They're in the business of acquiring good stuff or doing something new with the product. I assume that's the case. Are they in control of the market strategy? I don't know.

**MILLER:** I don't know if either of us could address that, because we both have peculiar relationships with publishers. Neither of us are hired guns in comics, so I don't know that I could answer that any better than you could.

**EISNER:** That's why I raised the question, because I don't know. The editors I deal with are the same ones you deal with. At DC, I deal with Karen Berger, who *acquired* me because she said yes to a book. For example, she looked at the dummy for *Fagin the Jew* and said, "We'd like to publish it." But I'm looking for a publisher with a special marketing capacity who will make what I hope will be a flurry of noise in the Jewish community. Somebody's gonna scream about this book. It's a polemic more than entertainment.[1]

**MILLER:** DC's a little problematic because they don't like noise. There's always been tension in my relationship with them because I want noise every time out.

**EISNER:** Their marketing system is a little different than that of the mainstream major publishing houses. Their history is comic books, and they are damn good at what they do. They're doing great with the *Spirit* collections. I'm happy.

**MILLER:** I'm hoping with the [Dark Horse] collection of P. Craig Russell's *Ring of the Nibelung,* an effort is made to reach the opera community.

**EISNER:** That's right, and a small publisher like Abrams, for instance — when I say small, I mean a *concentrated* publisher like Abrams — would make sure that every bookstore and every opera house around the country would have copies of this book.

..................................................................................................................
[1] *Fagin the Jew* was, in fact, published in 2003 by Doubleday, not DC.

But I don't think the big comics publishers *can* do that. They don't have the authority, they don't have the structure, they don't have the facilities to do that. They have "comics" tied to their name.

**MILLER:** No, they're selling the Bottled City of Kandor! They live in a world that doesn't exist and never did. This direct market[2] is a very strange and almost paranoid fantasy that publishers are in. They're not embracing the fact that we're part of a wider publishing and entertainment business, and making full use of it.

> "What the direct market regards as 'mainstream' is preposterous by normal human standards."

**EISNER:** They have to step out of the pattern. I don't agree with the idea that the direct market is a fantasy. It never was.

**MILLER:** The distribution system was a wonderful breakthrough, but I'm saying that what it regards as "mainstream" is preposterous by normal human standards.

**EISNER:** *[Laughs]* That's beautifully put, Frank, and you're right. [The real mainstream] is "uptown" from the direct market; it's the way the slaves looked at the white folks up on the hill. This is why I always say I want to be with the white folks up on the hill *[Miller laughs]*. It's a different marketplace, totally different, and it is part of a totally different kind of selling scheme. The reason, to answer your question, is that I think that people in big publishing houses like Marvel and DC have a problem of size. I don't know about Image … Dark Horse is flexible.

........................................................................................

[2] The "direct market" refers to the comics specialty shop distribution system largely pioneered by Phil Seuling in the seventies and still in force today.

**MILLER:** It would take Time-Warner's resources to really do it right.

**EISNER:** I don't think DC or Marvel have the structure. You would think, sitting here, that DC is a part of Time-Warner and so can get into places where nobody else can. Apparently, though, they're kept separate. I candidly don't know enough about the architecture of the Time-Warner publishing division.

**MILLER:** I think if I were to name the best and the worst thing that's happened to comics in my lifetime, it'd be the same sentence: The inmates took over the asylum *[Eisner laughs]*. A bunch of people who loved comics moved into it, which is great, but, unfortunately, its overall world is possessed with these fondly remembered childhood fantasies. To the point where you can do *The Name of the Game* or *A Contract with God,* I can go off and do *Sin City,* we can do anything we want to, and they'll smile at us and nod. But the minute I turn around and dent the Batmobile, they go out of their minds! They have such a precious view of these fantasies.

> "If I were to name the best and the worst thing that's happened to comics in my lifetime, it'd be the same sentence: The inmates took over the asylum."

**EISNER:** That's because you're working on a property that they have a lot invested in. When you're creating *Sin City,* it's your property. But they're lending you their car.

**MILLER:** Yeah, but they don't have any fun with it — come on!

**EISNER:** "You're borrowing my car; now, for goodness' sake, don't dent it!" *[Laughter]* This goes way back to Donenfeld's attitude, which was:

"My property is *Superman* and I own this property, so therefore I created it."[3]  After a while he believed he created it!  He used to run around in nightclubs.  He was a big nightclub-goer — here's this tiny little guy chasing after big, tall, fat blondes *[Miller laughs]* and wearing a T-shirt with a Superman emblem on it.

**MILLER:**  I take it all back.  The field hasn't changed a bit *[laughter]*!

> **"Comic book publisher Harry Donenfeld told the artists, as he told me, 'Look, I can replace you.'"**

**EISNER:**  Well, I don't see any of the current day publishers running around doing that … well, does Stan Lee still have a Rolls Royce?

**MILLER:**  Actually, they kick you out of Southern California after ten years if you don't have one.

**EISNER:**  Oh, is that right?!  *[Laughter]*

**MILLER:**  What you're talking about, what's resonant for me in my history in the field, is how disgraced a field it was.  It was the lower end.  I got into comics in the late seventies.  It was 1976 when I moved to Manhattan, and I was working by 1977.  You know how sometimes … I think we all have, in our history, that affair with the woman with low self-esteem who ends up being a lot of trouble because she holds herself in such low regard.  I felt that way about the people I met in comics.  I thought the best thing I could possibly be was a comic book artist.  And

[3] In 1937 Harry Donenfeld took over the fledgling Nartional Periodical Publications from Major Malcolm Wheeler-Nicholson and ran the company (later to be renamed DC Comics) until his death in 1965.

I was meeting these sad, hunched-over people who said, "What are you doing here?  Everybody knows there won't be any comic books in five years."  In the time I've been in the field, I've seen this self-loathing that seems to be so crippling.  When did that start?

**EISNER:**  It started with Harry Donenfeld at the beginning of DC.  It started way back in the forties and fifties.  Harry Donenfeld stood with me in an elevator one day and said, "I buy properties."  He said, "What do you mean you want to own this thing?  I own everything."  He was a tough little son-of-a-bitch.  "Look," he said to me, "I hire editors, and if the book doesn't sell, I fire the editors and get somebody else.  I can replace anybody I want in my shop."  He walked off the elevator, and that was the end of the conversation.

**MILLER:**  Carmine Infantino [renowned artist and former DC publisher] once said the same thing to me.

**EISNER:**  Carmine Infantino was part of the early structure.  Remember that the comic book publisher Harry Donenfeld resented everybody else

**The notorious "Donny Harrifield,"** from *The Dreamer*. © *1986 Will Eisner*

**Eisner's take on publishers Jack Liebowitz and Harry Donenfeld, from _The Dreamer_. © 1986 Will Eisner.**

coming into the business. He told the artists, as he told me, "Look, I can replace you." As a matter of fact, the artists working in the field in the late thirties and early forties would not talk to each other about their work for fear that they might be replaced.

I started teaching about the same time you got into the field, and I told my students they were going to write. And they all said, "No, I don't have to, because when I get a job they're gonna give me a writer." They were told from the very beginning that you are an "inker" or a "penciller." Period. What was happening was the animation concept was taking a grip on this business because of the kind of work and the speed at which it had to be turned out. *You* changed things very tremendously, you and maybe Gil Kane, but more you than anybody else changed things in the industry, because what you've done is you've developed an identity. The big change that occurred in this business, for artists, is that publishers began selling people, not things. Miller, [Neal] Adams, Gil Kane, Kirby, and so on.

> **"The big change that occurred in this business, for artists, is that publishers began selling people, not things."**

**MILLER:** I like to say the big mistake they made was putting our names on the books *[laughs]*!

**EISNER:** No, that was the only way they could survive. They did what I had talked to Stan Lee's boss about, and he didn't understand what the hell I was talking about — or maybe he did understand, and didn't want to listen because it meant giving up some profits.

# 15.....

# LIVING HISTORY

*The next morning, the two artists return to Eisner's studio and begin their discussion about the history of the comics business.*

**MILLER:** In the time I've been in the field, one of the most significant things that's happened is that stuff has come back into print. All of a sudden we have an *accessible* history of comics. If you go to a shop, you're looking at all the years of comics being represented, rather than just this one.

**EISNER:** I hadn't realized that. I thought I was no longer part of the "comic book" business. At least, I hoped not.

**MILLER:** I saw that starting to happen with *A Contract with God,* when you brought the concept of a permanent space on the shelves. I knew that

**Opposite: By reprinting every installment of *The Spirit* in the handsome archival format, DC Comics provides today's reader with access to a critical part of comics history. © 1946, 2003 Will Eisner**

would be the *best* thing for the future of comics — in fact, the only workable future. The only one that makes any sense. Now we have a *past*.

**EISNER:** This is interesting to me because, for me, we didn't have a past. We weren't conscious of it as a history. When you came into the field during the seventies, we already had thirty, forty years of existence, of building a thing.

> ## "All of a sudden we have an *accessible* history of comics."

**MILLER:** I hope the field becomes better informed and less reverent. There's too much bad work getting too much respect, but there's not enough knowledge of what makes comics work or worth doing. When the Warren [magazine] editions of *The Spirit* came out, it was just a shocking experience to me. I had seen one *Spirit* job in Feiffer's book [*The Comic Book Heroes*, 1965], but I had no idea of the scale of the series, or what you'd accomplished with it.

I remember going, "Oh, that's where Jim Steranko got his ideas. Cool!"

But those are the editions I relate to the most. It was just, like, this was done *when*? It was *cutting edge*; it was the best stuff around.

**EISNER:** Well …

**MILLER:** So I got my first real taste of history that wasn't from the two big houses [Marvel and DC].

**EISNER:** That's very interesting *[laughs]*. It's a little hard for me to talk about myself in public *[laughs]*.

**MILLER:** *The Spirit* had some effect on *Daredevil* that a few people noticed *[chuckles]*! I really do think it's a real boost for our field. And I wasn't the only one who felt that way; so did my peers in New York, who were also coming in [to the field].

New York was fascinating in the late seventies. There was a salon-like feel to it. We were paid like dogs, but it was a great time to work in comic books. Yes, the publishers owned everything. Yes, we got no royalties. But we all had lunch together, we were always trying to top each other, it was a wonderful time.

**EISNER:** I remember, in the fifties, sitting in a train coming in from White Plains [New York], with other artists — neighbors. They didn't talk shop, they didn't tell each other what they were doing. I sat on this train with another cartoonist who worked at one of the major houses, and I said, "What are you doing?" And he said, "I'm not going to tell any other guy what I'm working on! You might steal it." I told him, "Sure, they can take your idea, but they'll not do the idea the way you'll do it." So, to another guy sitting there I said, "What are you working on now?" And he said, "Something new," and changed the subject.

I tried very hard to bring about a salon system here, which I'd found, in Europe, was a wonderful thing. Sitting in a café somewhere, smoking, drinking, and bitching about the publishers …

**MILLER:** The usual stuff.

**EISNER:** The usual stuff. But, there, they talked openly about what they were doing; they boasted about what they were doing. And you had the chance of being able to hear what another guy was working on and to measure yourself against the competition. You guys loved the medium. Nobody I started with except Will Eisner had the temerity to admit that he loved the medium and that he would spend the rest of his life doing it.

**MILLER:**  It's changed a lot, but there's still a lot to change.  I got more respect for writing bad movies than I ever did for writing a comic book.[1] That told me a lot about the field and its self-regard.  I do think that there's a rather dramatic generational shift going on.  I think there are people coming in who don't carry that baggage.

**EISNER:**  But the point I'm making is that the feeling cartoonists have about their own business is promoted by the culture itself.  We are still regarded as a low art.  On top there's oil painting, then there's etching, there's wood engraving, there's silkscreen, and finally there's comics.

> "Nobody I started with except Will Eisner had the temerity to admit that he loved the medium and that he would spend the rest of his life doing it."

**MILLER:**  Yeah — there's dead, not quite dead, still kind of breathing, and alive and ugly!

**EISNER:**  That's right.  Why does a guy who paints on a wall or does oil on canvas, why is what he's doing "Fine" Art, and why is what Frank Miller's doing *not* Fine Art?

**MILLER:**  Because I really do believe that something's got to have coughed up its last and been lying there a long time before it gains any respect.  I think we are in a young and vital form that has a rather dangerous outlaw aspect to it, and that's one of the things I love about it.

[1] Miller is referring primarily to his first stint in Hollywood, in the eighties.

**EISNER:** What I'm getting at is what you ran into when you came into this field: the slave mentality.

**MILLER:** Absolutely.

**EISNER:** You get a slave and you tell him, "Look, you can't go anywhere; the best you can do is shine shoes." And the slave says to his kid, "Learn how to shine shoes; that's as far as you can go."

**MILLER:** One of the things that makes you such a strange figure in the history of comics, Will, is that you've so much set your own course that you aren't a part of this. But when I came in, it was considered a matter of ethical virtue to act like a slave. It was considered arrogant and uppity and vaguely traitorous to stand a little too tall.

**EISNER:** In 1940 I gave an interview with the *Baltimore Sun* when *The Spirit* first came out, and I said, "This is a literary art form." And the guys were laughing at me and said, "What are you trying to prove, Will, who do you think you are?" [Newspaper cartoonist] Rube Goldberg told me what I was saying was bullshit. He said, "Shit, boy, you're a vaudevillian. Don't forget this is vaudeville."

> **"We are in a young and vital form that has a rather dangerous outlaw aspect to it, and that's one of the things I love about it."**

Milton Caniff, he believed in me, but in the [*Shop Talk*] interview with Milt when I said, "Milt, you're a great writer, I admire your work." He said, "Oh, I sell papers." And nobody in the National Cartoonists Society would admit that he was anything more than a [news]paper seller. They regarded themselves as entertainers.

**MILLER:** You know, "entertainer" is fine in my book. What I won't take is "factory hand." I'm convinced the reason the division of labor has gotten so broad among comic book publishers like Marvel and DC — where they have pencillers, inkers, scripters, letterers, and all that — is that it's the only way they can justify the utterly indefensible legal position about work-made-for-hire.

**EISNER:** No, I disagree with you there. The reason for that [division of labor] is the quantity of stuff that has to get done. Just think of how many books a month DC and Marvel put out. There's no way ... I'm fast, I do a page a day, but in thirty days the best I can do is thirty pages — if I don't go to the bathroom *[Miller laughs]*. And to write it ... writing a book normally takes me maybe three to four weeks, a month to write. The publisher has got to turn out lots of books. He can't afford to deal with someone who just writes and draws at the same time, and the guy who writes and draws at the same time can't make enough money, even if he's getting $300 a page — which is what I think they're paying now, maybe more.

**MILLER:** I gave up on page rates a long time ago.

**EISNER:** I'm not talking about you, I'm talking about the average guy. The average guy who's working in the field can barely turn out a page a day — maybe it takes him two days to do a page. So he's winding up with maybe $600 or $800 a week. Well, that's about $35,000 to $45,000 a year, and that ain't a hell of a lot of money these days. I'm talking *average*!

**MILLER:** I guess in a way we're both talking like we're two cousins in a dysfunctional family whose relatives keep jumping out of buildings and we're wondering why.

**EISNER:** Your reason is the house got too small and this guy jumped out — and I'm saying no, wait a minute, it's something deeper than that. I've been around a lot longer, and I've seen a lot more.

**MILLER:** What's fascinating to see, though, is right now there's an entire new crop of artists coming into comics, and to their eyes I may as well have been doing comics in the thirties, because these artists are so fresh and they're coming in so wild-eyed with stuff that's just shocking in its clarity. Not everything's good — most of it's pretty awful, but there's a sense of joy they're bringing in that doesn't seem tainted by the work-for-hire publisher.

**EISNER:** If you go down to that Washington [D.C.] show ...

**MILLER:** SPX? It's a great show.

**EISNER:** Yeah. Stand on your toes when you're looking at the work. Don't look at it closely. There's a field of flowers blooming. Each of these guys ... some of them were showing me stuff that made me want to cry. This boy showed me this stuff that came right out of his heart, out of his gut. The art was absolutely primitive. But what he was saying ... wow!

**MILLER:** But isn't it wonderful to see people who are so unprejudiced that they'll break rules? And sometimes you realize they're right, that it works.

**EISNER:** What does that say to you?

**MILLER:** Well, it reminds me of myself as a boy who folded over typing paper and stapled it together and drew a comic.

**EISNER:** What it says to me is that here is a medium that's providing a vehicle for that kind of expression. It always had that, but now, because of guys like you — because of Art Spiegelman, because of Scott McCloud, Chris Ware, guys like that — that's why these people have turned to this medium as a vehicle. There was this feeling before ... in 1935 when I started, there were people walking around with the same internal feelings, the same heartbreak, the same angst, but there was no

**In addition to Miller, Eisner also credits other innovators like Art Spiegelman, Scott McCloud, and Chris Ware as inspiring a new generation of more alternative, less commercially oriented cartoonists.** *Photo by Charles Brownstein.*

place else to do it. Maybe the great pulp magazines, but here suddenly is a field that will accept this thing. This is why I think this business is just beginning. That's why I wish I were 25 or thirty years younger. As a matter of fact, the only thing that makes me envious is that I went into the valley before anybody else, and now everybody's coming into the valley and building things all around me.

Anyway, the point I'm making is: change your outlook, Frank. The situation is not as dire as you think it is.

**MILLER:** I don't think it's dire. I think there's a deep-seated sickness.

**EISNER:** That sounds dire. A deep-seated sickness is pretty goddamn dire to me!

**From the Pulitzer-winning *Maus*.** © *1986, 1989, 1990, 1991 Art Spiegelman*

**From *Acme Novelty Library*.**
© *2001-2002 Chris Ware*

**From the seminal
*Understanding Comics*.**
© *1993 Scott McCloud*

**MILLER:** I'm just trying to address something that has to do with our history.

**EISNER:** What is the sickness?

**MILLER:** The sickness is self-contempt. I am the young puppy of a certain generation that started becoming a force in comics in the seventies and eighties, but I still see the industry of comics hobbled by this sense of worthlessness that thinks of the medium as a genre that'll be shaken off over time. It still amazes me how deep-rooted that is.

**EISNER:** I see what you're saying, and my vision stays with the fact that here is a medium that's providing a vehicle for a good kind of thing. I don't think it'll destroy the medium.

**MILLER:** No, I don't either. I get impatient. I imagine at times you've gotten impatient. What I'm saying is that comics has this history of shame. I just wonder how much poison was left in this system during the fifties. The Comics Code still hangs over us like a Sword of Damocles. It won't go away.

**EISNER:** It's long outlived its usefulness. What exactly is the point you raise? How much an early attitude towards this medium — this shame, as you've talked about — has remained? Maybe a lot of it has remained. There's a lot of it still. In the fifties there was still a feeling of shame in doing comics. But remember, I was on a different side of the street. The only things I heard were secondhand. I can't tell you what was going on then in the comic book community, among the comic book artists, because I was not a part of it. I was working in a totally different field, selling the comics medium to industries who were buying the use of comics because it was a novelty. That's a totally different thing. During World War II I worked on a magazine called *Army Motors*, and then in 1950, during the Korean War, they came back and asked if I'd be interested in re-creating that magazine. At that time I was a civilian, so

**Connie Redd gives
soldiers tips on
tank maintenance.
From issue #125 of
*P.S. Magazine*, an
instructional comic
Eisner developed
for the U.S. Army.**
*Published in 1963
by the Department
of the Army.*

we negotiated a contract so I could be a private contractor.  So the army stuff was different.  It was instructional comics, not comic books.

But you said something earlier that I'd like to get back to.  I'd like to put in my candidacy for being one of the people in the field who has spent his entire life trying to improve the medium itself.  I like to think that because of that, these people now have a vehicle with which they can express themselves.

The people who are feeling the self-contempt that you're talking about are people who are clones, who probably have no vision of what their self-worth is or what they want to say.

# 16.......

# PUBLISHERS
# AND OUTLAWS

**MILLER:** I don't think my point of view is as dire as I'm coming across to you. I think what I'm attacking here is the attitude that perhaps more than anybody else the major publishers still seem to behave like a scared little kid looking at his comic books under the covers with a flashlight and hoping his mother won't find him. There's still a sense of "don't notice me."

**EISNER:** Let's define publishers. A publisher is a marketer. He is looking to supply something to a market. His main function is to find a market for whatever property he has or to find someone to provide him with a product to satisfy a market.

**MILLER:** Say what you want about Hugh Hefner, but he is a publisher and he has a vision.

Opposite: From *A Contract with God.* © 1978 Will Eisner

**Publishers are essentially marketers, according to Eisner.** From *The Dreamer*.
© *1986 Will Eisner*

..................................................................................................

**EISNER:** Yeah, but he had a market and he sold to that market.

**MILLER:** Bill Gaines.

**EISNER:** Bill Gaines was something else again. Bill Gaines inherited something; he didn't build it. Harvey Kurtzman had the vision; Bill Gaines had the money and the property. Gaines had the vision of taking cartoonists out to parties overseas *[Miller laughs]*. I'm sorry to do this to you, but it's good for you, because you've got good ideas and someone who thinks the way you do should be informed and know exactly what the situation is.

The function of a publisher is to find a market. They're in pursuit of a readership; that's what their job is. And along comes a Frank Miller. They didn't invent Frank Miller. No one told you what direction to go in, but suddenly you came along and the audience said, "Yeah, Frank!" and the publisher said, "Yeah, Frank!" Before you, there weren't too many guys who had their name above the title.

Don't expect from publishers something that they cannot give or have no intention of giving.

**MILLER:** Why be ashamed of ourselves? That's a fault of the business, perpetrated not just by the publishers but also by the talent.

In the early eighties, a colleague of mine got a prose novel published. And one of the top people at Marvel Comics turned to me and said, "As of today, this guy's a giant and we're ants because he's a real writer." Jesus Christ! His book was remaindered by Berkley *[Eisner laughs]*!

"Whether publishers are interested in art or not, publishers are to be respected. They're the guys who understand marketing. They understand where to find an audience, how to find it, and how to exploit someone like you or someone like me. "

**EISNER:** Well, look, the point I'm making is that the medium you're working in is a very important medium. It's capable of providing a vehicle for expression for these very primitive emotions that these SPX people want to express. There is no other medium that they have access as quickly and as easily to, and that's the reason this medium will continue and grow. Now, whether publishers are interested in art or not, publishers are to be respected. They're the guys who understand marketing. They understand where to find an audience, how to find it, and how to exploit someone like you or someone like me. They understand how to do that. You or I haven't got the patience to do that. We haven't got the kind of thinking to do that. They do it very well. So don't lose sight of the fact that you are working in a very important medium. I believe in the future of this medium and think it will be tremendous. More tremendous than it's ever been. It may not be as profitable for publishers as it was, but I think it'll continue to grow.

**MILLER:** Still, I think that you've been painting a rosy portrait of what is a pretty rough-and-tumble, nasty business. Comics history is pretty brutal.

**EISNER:** Well, perhaps as a business. My relationships with people were a lot softer than you're talking about. But then I was not in the scrim[mage]. I was on the outside, and as I said earlier, no one ever laid a glove on me. Even in the business of fighting for ownership of *The Spirit*, I did it in a smart, businesslike way. It's what somebody referred to as business cunning — but actually, no, I followed a very simple principle in business, and I think that young people who want to manage their own business can take this advice: Any deal with anybody, regardless of whether it's business or other social relationships, has to be based on the fact that each guy is getting something from the deal. You cannot make a deal with somebody and ask him to do something that you know he cannot do. It's like average young students who come into the field and say, "I'm being screwed." Well, they're not being screwed. The guy's offering you a deal, and you can take it or leave it. Of course, publishers do have an access to distribution that you don't. But that's another thing.

**MILLER:** But that's kind of semantic, because the reality for most freelancers who got into comics over a decade ago was that there were two options: to let other people own their work at Marvel, or to let other people own their work at DC. There were a limited number of publishers, and the terms of the deal were pretty poor. They were so bad that, by the time I got in, the only people who *would* come in were the people who were still in love with comics. They were willing to do day jobs at advertising agencies to stay afloat.

> "Comics history is pretty brutal."

**EISNER:** That is a very important thing you're saying, because that is a very basic difference. Prior to that, it was a market like any other market. These were the prices that were being paid. I got five dollars a page in the beginning. Why? Not because a publisher was trying to screw me, but the publishers were trying to buy within what they thought the work was worth. The initial publishers, the pulp publishers, who had been buying proofs from the syndicates — the *Dick Tracy* proofs and so forth — were being charged five dollars for a week's worth of proofs. Which is the same price the syndicates were charging small, local newspapers for a week of *Dick Tracy*. So the publisher said, "The market price is what we're going to pay." The only thing that changes the price is the availability of the market. When you got into this business, there was a long history where the whole nature of the equation had turned around and changed. By the time you got into the business, publishers realized that it was not enough to own a property. It was more important to get the right guy, one who had a market. There was a market out there that needed a different kind of addressing. You could no longer survive on just owning *Superman* and having any idiot do *Superman*. It now depended on *who* was doing *Superman*.

> "Any deal with anybody, regardless of whether it's business or other social relationships, has to be based on the fact that each guy is getting something from the deal."

**MILLER:** I think that's still sinking in, to tell the truth. I believe there's almost an ethical investment in the notion that we're still replaceable. Sometimes I think that the work-made-for-hire mentality, which is what I'm really going to attack here, is deeply ingrained in our business. I'm not saying artists should give up *Superman* or *Batman*, because the deals have gotten significantly better, but after seeing my contemporaries, after knowing myself, and after seeing what guys older than me behave like, there's something that is damaging to people about not having territory

**Miller's take on Batman has always been revolutionary. From volume 3 of *DK2*. © 2002 DC Comics**

over their own work. I think it eats away at the soul — and has, with a lot of people in the field.

**EISNER:** Well, that's pretty broad and it's very dramatic. I'm choking back a tear.

**MILLER:** Oh, come on! It's gotta be said.

**EISNER:** Okay, Frank, look, it *is* destructive to somebody's sense of self-worth if he doesn't own something, but in place of that there's also a sense of self-worth in your ability to do something and get paid for it. Your conversation is an exercise of your being aware of the fact that you have a skill — and a very marketable skill. You aren't talking about what you own or the properties you own, you're talking about Frank Miller's ability to take an old property like *Batman* and, with your own skill and your own particular type of vision, make it something other than just what it was. The publisher loaned you *Batman* because you are Frank Miller, and you promised to rejuvenate a property that was losing its value. It was at that point, in my opinion, that the whole psychology, the nature of the thinking by the owners of these properties, changed. When I started, the attitude of comic book publishers was very much like [that of] the animation business. You were an in-betweener, an inker, and "I own Mickey Mouse." Everybody else was working within the frame of Mickey Mouse, and nobody had any equity in that.

[Harry] Donenfeld was fierce about the fact that he had an equity and he had a property and he had a command of the industry. But everybody else … going back to what you were talking about with the so-called soul of the cartoonist, what was happening is what I referred to before as the slave mentality. Maybe that's where we can agree: that there was a slave mentality in the business, and the guy who was working on *Superman,* or any one of the superheroic characters who came afterwards, was working on a property that was owned by somebody else.

**MILLER:** I guess the point that I want to make clear is that I hardly regard myself as a victim. I've enjoyed the work-for-hire stuff I've done, and I enjoy it when I do it. But I'm sure glad that I don't do it most of the time. I'm glad that I do things that I own and where I have no boss. But I do believe that, over a long period of time, being that kind of hired gun is not good for an artist and is not good for the art form.

**EISNER:** Why did you go back to Batman this time? You didn't really have to. You can do other things.

**MILLER:** I really wanted to. I had a fun story, and I didn't want to come up with my own [creator-owned] version of a Batman. I might as well play with that toy if that's what I'm thinking of anyway. And I'm being well rewarded for it.

**EISNER:** Is that the reason, because you're being well rewarded?

**MILLER:** No. I wouldn't have waited fifteen years if that were the reason. The reason I mentioned I was well rewarded was so I wouldn't sound like I was a victim.

**EISNER:** No, no, you're not. The question I'm asking you is: Where do you think you're going? You're at the fifty-yard line of your life; what is there yet that you think you have to do?

**MILLER:** Right now, year by year, something bugs me enough to tell me it's something I'm gonna do.

**EISNER:** You're not walking around with a long-term vision floating over your head?

**MILLER:**  No, what I'm focusing on now are the stories I'm working on, obviously.  And also trying to think if there's anything I'd like to do in a broader sense in the comics industry — beyond trying to cure some of the stupid, bad habits of that awful format that hasn't made sense since comics cost a dime — to help make comics a much more cocky and proud member of popular culture, rather than an obscure thing that focuses on nostalgia for characters that were made up sixty years ago.

**EISNER:**  It is not yet cocky enough, I agree.  But I don't want you to make this a cocky medium.  I want this medium to come up and live with the white folks on the hill.  As far as being cocky, abrasive, revolutionary … we were revolutionary long ago.  The medium is no longer a novelty unto itself.  There was a time when I could sell a comic to General Motors simply because it was comics.

**MILLER:**  I disagree.  I think that comics are at their best when they are provocative, and their outlaw nature is what I want to seek out in them. We have a form that does not have the visceral, technical power of film. It's up to the reader to control the time.  It's essentially a cold medium, which means that it can carry more and more outrageous ideas.  Also, it's an infinite medium, which means you or I can sit down and make a comic, and we don't need to be bankrolled by a movie studio.  I like to use it for that.

**EISNER:**  We're arguing over semantics.  When you say comics, I think of comics as a medium.  It's a vehicle with which one can do what you call outrageous things and create new and unusual ideas.  But the medium itself, the business of arranging images in an intelligent sequence to tell an idea or a story, has long since stopped being a novelty as a medium.

**MILLER:**  It's definitely been proven as an art form; I don't think we need to plead that case anymore.  We don't need to keep rationalizing our existence.  Now I think we're on the offensive, culturally.  We hit the ground running, and we've fed all the other parts of our contemporary culture with various ideas and thanked them for taking them for us.

And at the same time — and this is where I really fault my generation of cartoonists, and, up until fairly recently, myself included — is that we have not been absorbing enough of the really exciting stuff that's happening along the fringes of culture. There's been a revolution in fashion, in commentary, in satire, and I want us to be a part of this crazy mix that's going on.

> ## "I want this medium to come up and live with the white folks on the hill."

**EISNER:** Okay, but what I want to ask your generation is: Where are you going? My generation didn't know where it was going. Yes, I was walking around saying, "Charge! Let's take that hill up there!" But your generation didn't seem to have that kind of thing, from where I stood. When you came along I was already established, I'd gone past the revolution, I'd placed a stake in the beachhead and said, "This is where I think we're going," or "This is where I want us to go." I didn't know if anybody would follow me. But eventually a bunch of guys did follow me, Spiegelman and so on. But what you guys were doing, you particularly, was taking an existing medium and moving it forward, changing it in some way. But nobody in your generation, that I knew of, had any vision of the future. They weren't going anywhere with this thing; they were going to do what they were doing, but better.

**MILLER:** *[Stands from his chair and steps backwards.]* This is how we moved into the future! At least one rift among many I see in my field — and this is not a generational rift entirely — is that an awful lot of people in comics are far too reverent to the comics they grew up with and far too willing to play to what didn't work, and what doesn't work, than to come up with something new. I keep making reference to curators. It's like they're dusting off these old toys. We've got a vital, lovely form.

**EISNER:** I felt sorry for you guys. I looked at Frank Miller, or the other Frank Millers, and I said to myself, "Holy Christ, these guys are sitting here with an already established marketplace." And many of your contemporaries were working off the old stuff, regurgitating the old stuff over and over again. That was what was happening early. Even at Marvel and DC, people there were regurgitating stuff that had existed before.

**MILLER:** They still are.

**EISNER:** I was looking at you guys and I felt luckier, because when I started there was nothing behind us. What we were bringing into the field were things we had learned from the great classics — Robert Louis Stevenson, people of that sort. This is what we could work off, and we brought it into the field. Or the daily strips. But as far as superheroes were concerned, that was an introduction that was already there when you guys came along. I remember that students in my class were doing superheroes. I kept saying to them, "Don't do any superheroes!" They were wasting their time struggling for new costumes. They said that that was the market.

Comics pioneers like Eisner had no prior generation of comics artists to look to for inspiration and instead were influenced by classic adventure novelists, such as Robert Louis Stevenson. From Eisner's *Hawks of the Seas*.
© 1986, 2003 Denis Kitchen

**MILLER:** But, Will, this ties into what I was saying about the way the field was at that time. I showed up in New York naively with a whole bunch of pages that were a primitive version of *Sin City*. They were crime stories, and nobody was in tights at all. And people looked at me like I was completely nuts, because there was only one kind of comic book being published. So superheroes *were* the place to start.

> "There seem to be people who really do regard themselves as custodians of these published legends. Other people think we'll go Hollywood and we'll all be fabulously rich. After a while you realize that the first is stupid and the other is questionable."

**EISNER:** So, in order to make a foothold in the field, you accommodated to that and began doing the kinds of things that the publishers wanted.

**MILLER:** I took what they had and did my crime stories with tights.

**EISNER:** Later on.

**MILLER:** No, with *Daredevil*. I was taking over a character …

**EISNER:** The early *Daredevils* that I saw that you did were very much like what was the standard. It was only later that you began to grow out of it.

**MILLER:** They were quite shocking to a lot of the audience. You don't know how reverent this audience is to old comic books.

**Miller would transpose his early crime stories — and characters — into his later professional work for Marvel.** ©*1976 Frank Miller, Inc.*

**EISNER:** Is that right?

**MILLER:** That's why I keep harping on it. There seem to be people who really do regard themselves as custodians of these published legends. Other people think we'll go Hollywood and we'll all be fabulously rich. After a while you realize that the first is stupid and the other is questionable. What I see is a much more rational approach where we recognize that we are part of popular culture, but we also recognize that we will never be able to compete with mass media. We basically need a more intelligent and daring reader than someone who just goes to the movies and watches television. I see us as growing, but in a measured, sensible way. Not the sudden rapture that the Hollywood freaks keep predicting.

**EISNER:** I agree with that and will repeat myself that I feel we are now a valid medium. We are no longer a novelty, so therefore what the new writer has to do, working in this medium, is come up with story material that is more relevant to our thinking.

**MILLER:** I think from now on we should stop arguing that we're valid. We just *are*. Let them react to it. That's why I said "cocky." We need to stop trying to convince people. We're right. They'll catch on.

> **"I think from now on we should stop arguing that we're valid. We just *are*."**

**EISNER:** This brings us to the question I asked before, which is: Where do you see this going? People keep asking me that question, and now I'm at the point that I'm convinced that we have to do more of what we've always done. I'm talking about the cutting-edge people, the Chris Wares and the Art Spiegelmans.

**MILLER:** Right, and now that we are developing a growing library of work that crosses the whole period of comics history, I'd like to see it continue to grow — but no buying new shelves. I think we can start thinning the herd as more good stuff comes in. I don't think we need to be doting over stuff that somebody bombed out in ten minutes in 1942.

**EISNER:** You can be sure of one thing, Frank. The work being done from here on in, ninety percent of it will be crap.

**MILLER:** Sure, and that would be a real upgrade!

# 17.·····

# SHOP TALK

**EISNER:** I could never work with somebody else.

**MILLER:** But you used to run a shop!

**EISNER:** I ran a shop, but that's a totally different thing. That's like running a school.

**MILLER:** How did it work? Did you lay out the stories?

**EISNER:** In the Eisner & Iger days, I'd start off a story by creating a character, setting up the plot, and then giving the artists a drawing. For instance, I drew the first cover of *Sheena*.

**MILLER:** Was the shop the image that we all have, of a room full of people behind their boards?

**EISNER:** It was very much like a workshop, in the Eisner & Iger period. Later, it was an apartment in Tudor City [New York], and there were six guys in two rooms. As you came in, there was a living room and a bedroom. The bedroom was my office. It had my drawing board and everything else in there. And then in the main room there were five guys: Chuck Cuidera on one side of the door, Bob Powell, Lou Fine, Tex Blaisdell, and Chuck Mazoujian.

> "Jerry Iger was a real go-getter.
> He was like a little fighting cock."

**MILLER:** Wow.

**EISNER:** They were all sitting in, that way. And I would walk in and we would talk. See, I hit on a very good idea with Eisner & Iger, and it worked very beautifully for me. Everybody else was buying artwork on a per-page basis. I said, "No, I'm going to pay a salary." Y'see, it gave me better control over quality. [Jerry] Iger and I used to fight over that; he was furious with me about that. He thought it was a risky method of production.

I learned a lot of business from Iger. He was hard to live with, but I learned a lot about business. He was a real go-getter. He was like a little fighting cock. He'd go out there, and he'd call on anybody. He'd call on the President of the United States! At nineteen years old, I couldn't bring myself to do that kind of thing. But the salary was a very cunning and very good idea. It worked. If you've got a guy sitting in your shop and you're paying him by the page and you say to him, "That's no good, change that," he's going to blow your head off. But in my shop I could go to Bob Powell and say, "Bob, that doesn't work, change it." And he'd say, "Sure, I don't care, I'll get my salary on Friday either way." Jack Kirby would do the same thing. Jack was very amenable.

I ran my shop very much like a class, like running a school.

**MILLER:** But you were a foreman!

**EISNER:** I was the player-manager. Then I'd go back and sit at the drawing board to do my thing.

**MILLER:** When you came in, how many people did you know who were working in comics because that was their passion, because they wanted to do comics?

**EISNER:** Nobody had a passion. *I* was the only guy I knew who believed that this was a lifetime career. The rest of them were working to

**In the early days of the industry, working in comics was not thought of as an end in itself. From *The Dreamer*. © *1986 Will Eisner***

make enough money so they could go *uptown*. They dreamed of going up Madison Avenue and becoming illustrators. Their dream was to do illustrations for the *Saturday Evening Post*, things like that.

**MILLER:** Those were great venues for illustrators.

**EISNER:** Yeah. They were. Some of the illustrators were like movie stars; they were making big, big money. Lou Fine went into illustration. He didn't want to be a comics professional. Chuck Mazoujian became an art director and spent the rest of his life, after he left my shop, working in advertising agencies, doing illustration. There was a company called Johnstone and Cushing that produced promotional comics. You must remember, in those days the standard was good illustration, good drawing, good draftsmanship. Lou Fine was ideal for that because his draftsmanship was so superb.

Today they look around and say, "I want to be like Frank Miller; his stuff is in movies." There's always the hope of a movie deal. The publishers are running around with hopes of a movie deal. They're looking at new stuff that they're getting and hoping they can sell it to the movies. A lot of publishers are selling comics properties to movies.

**MILLER:** Here I've got to get back to what we were talking about earlier. I came in as one of that generation who honestly wanted to do comic books. We were in love with the damn things. We came in with that as our ambition. You were surrounded by a bunch of people who basically regarded themselves as *not* doing their chosen profession. I came in with a bunch of people who grew up reading comic books and were in love with them. Our day job was often advertising. We did some pretty crappy advertising work! Neal Adams's Continuity Associates was a real halfway house for all of us; he would give us grunt work and we got, like, ten bucks an hour, and comics became something people did almost as an avocation. That was a time when people really were in comics for no reason other than love of the medium.

**EISNER:** That's a very important point. There was a period where I suddenly became aware of the fact that there were people who really wanted to do this as a vocation. Up until then, there was about a 25-year period where I was really out of the comic book scene. I was not interested. I didn't want to do comic books; I was doing my own thing. But what you're talking about is a very interesting definition of the climate, in terms of where this business has gone.

Think about it. In 1942, everybody in the comics business was doing it *only* because it was a way to make a living.

**MILLER:** *[Laughs]* Yeah, and in my generation they were doing it despite the fact that it was not a way to make money.

**EISNER:** In your generation they recognized the medium as a valid medium for them.

**MILLER:** Well, a lot of them were just in love with *Spider-Man* or some such. There was that infantile appeal, too.

**EISNER:** We had no precedent. We came along, and there were twenty or thirty years where comics were ordinary. We could not look at the work and think, "This stinks; I think I can do something better here." We had nothing to measure against. All we had were daily newspaper strips.

**MILLER:** There was no "before you."

**EISNER:** There was no "before" for my generation. That's one of the reasons why a lot of creative stuff was coming, because we were bringing into the field things from other media. *Hawks of the Seas* was simply a rip-off of [Rafael] Sabatini's pirate stories. Lou Fine and I were crazy about magazine illustration.

**MILLER:** Howard Pyle must have been open on a lot of desks.

**Early 20th-century author Rafael Sabatini served as the primary inspiration for Eisner's *Hawks of the Seas*. © 1986, 2003 Denis Kitchen**

**EISNER:**  Howard Pyle, N.C. Wyeth, and other illustrators.  Then there were pulp magazine illustrators —

**MILLER:**  They were *terrific*.

**EISNER:**  But these were illustrations that had nothing to do with the storytelling quality.  When you came along, it was like a plant that had been growing alongside a rock somewhere and now it had roots …

**MILLER:**  It had roots, but unfortunately it was growing under a table!

**EISNER:**  It was still a questionable art form, but it had reached a point where it was a valid, recognizable, measurable medium.

**MILLER:** What really honks me off is that as bad as things were in the thirties, I still feel that something happened with the fifties, with the Kefauver Hearings, that cast a shadow over the business of comics, which has yet to lift.

**EISNER:** Hmm. I don't know.

**MILLER:** That's why I make reference to the girl with low self-esteem who you might have had an affair with in your twenties. There's this weird thing that has haunted this field for generations now. When I first came in, during the late seventies, there was this constant sense that we were the "niggers" of entertainment — and I think that persists and hasn't progressed.

**EISNER:** You're quite right that the fifties reinforced the prejudice that existed before then. But what happened was the guys began doing good things, like Kurtzman, to try to break away in their own way. It wasn't until the underground comix, in the seventies, that people really began doing what I considered literature. That's really what propelled me back into the field.

**MILLER:** Precisely because it was so outlaw.

**EISNER:** More than that, Frank. What they were doing was addressing real social values, for the first time. The artwork was in many cases just pure, primitive art, and the writing was very ridiculous, but they were addressing a social problem with this medium. They were using the medium as a literary form. Before that, comics had been used as an entertainment form, which is the way comics had always been regarded. They'd always been an entertainment form. I think those are the big changes.

**MILLER:** Earlier you spoke about how primitive the new stuff popping up is. I think, as craftsmen, we need a steady dose of what we may call "primitive" stuff popping up, to remind us of what we do for a living — that, as artists, there's a purity in the act of conveying information in a single line that one begins to lose as one falls in love with illustration.

One of the things I like about the undergrounds, and that I like about what's going on right now [with small-press comics], is people are getting right back down to the bone marrow of what comics are, and I need to see that to refresh myself.

**EISNER:** When you talk about comic book art, do you see it as separate from the story?

**MILLER:** No.

> **"It wasn't until the underground comix, in the seventies, that people really began doing what I considered literature."**

**EISNER:** Because what you have is a dominance in some periods of people with a very primitive art style but with very sophisticated ideas. What you're seeing now [in the alternative press] are sophisticated ideas with primitive art, where when I started we had sophisticated art with very primitive ideas.

**MILLER:** Yeah, like Lou Fine drawing *Captain Marvel Jr.*

**EISNER:** Up until the seventies in San Francisco among all these "heads," nobody had used comics to do anything more than to entertain. These guys were attacking the Establishment in an entertaining way …

**MILLER:** It was quite entertaining.

**EISNER:** I don't wring my hands over what I call primitive art, because I no longer have the preoccupation with drawing style. Remember, I grew up when good drawing was regarded as the apex of our work. If it was well drawn, everybody would say that was enough. Now, the *ideas* are what's important. You get guys like Tom Toles doing a daily —

**MILLER:** He's a brilliant cartoonist.

**EISNER:** He's a cartoonist, but his style looks primitive.

**MILLER:** Yeah, he can't do a caricature to save his life, but he's one of the best editorial cartoonists in the country.

**EISNER:** He has ideas, and it's his ideas that are really important.

**MILLER:** He replaced Herblock in the *Washington Post* . . .

**EISNER:** Is he the one who just did this [strip] that created all the problems, where he attacked the [victims' kin] post-9/11?

**MILLER:** No, you're thinking of Ted Rall.

**EISNER:** Ted Rall, sorry.

**MILLER:** Ted Rall is a whole other case. He can't draw either, and it doesn't slow him down much because his ideas are very good.

It's interesting, because I can see how so much of your generation did come from Howard Pyle and all. There was such a sense of craftsmanship.

My generation, in many ways, was plainly dominated by Neal Adams. He was the guy who came in and put photorealism in comics. He was about the only interesting guy in his generation. Neal was this big, powerful force. Creatively, he shocked everybody, because all of a sudden you opened up a comic book and there'd be a character who had wings — and they were real wings! We went gaga. All of us little kids felt that *reality* had finally reached us. Neal's influence reached its apotheosis, or catastrophic finish, with Alex Ross's stuff.

**Neal Adams brought a love of finish and illustrative quality to his artwork, according to Miller. From *The Brave and the Bold* #79, with inks by Dick Giordano.** © *1968 DC Comics*

Neal was the dominant guy in terms of business and creative issues. A lot of us would simply go hang out at his studio. He was looking over my portfolio for years before I got any work. He would give me all the time in the world. But he brought this love of finish and illustrative quality that, in many ways, I've been spending a good chunk of my career trying to get rid of, because I think the hang-up of draftsmanship got carried away, and cartooning got lost in the mix. Not in his own work, because Neal's a fine cartoonist, but the people who imitated him just stuffed their heads up their asses.

**EISNER:** The preoccupation with the *quality* of the art dominated this medium, from a professional practitioner point of view, up until the seventies. It persists in many ways, even through to *Spawn,* which sells itself on its artwork. There's no content to it, but it sells itself on the excitement of its artwork. There's a seductiveness about the style of it, apparently, that's brought [Todd McFarlane] lots of readers.

**MILLER:** Neal brought back the *line;* he really did. Things had simply become hackwork, by and large. The only guy who was perfect technically was Kirby, and Kirby's stuff wasn't exactly encouraging draftsmanship. It was brilliant stuff, but he was almost the first postmodern cartoonist or something, because his art was so abstract. Then Neal Adams came charging in, and he really did bring a level of finish that blew everybody's mind. I think his impact in history will be interesting to note, because it was ultimately short-lived but very deep.

**EISNER:** That's an interesting point. Every thought I have is modified with a bunch of adjectives and adverbs because I'm still awed about where this medium has gone.

**MILLER:** Well, I think it's really strange that we're talking about an art form that had a very stunted, strange development, but it's just getting started.

**EISNER:** Exactly.

**MILLER:** I don't think either of us can see where it's gonna go; we just want to have fun getting as far as we will with it.

**EISNER:** Well, if we could see where it's going to go, we would be ... Look, in 1972, '74, '75, I thought I could see where it was going. It didn't go there that fast; it took some twenty-odd years to get there, and what's only happening now I thought would happen overnight. I thought that if I published *A Contract with God,* that would break through and there would be hordes of publishers coming in.

**MILLER:**  And I thought as soon as we got royalties and some of the rights, we'd have this creative renaissance.  When we could own the material and get our fair share of the money made from it, I thought there'd be an absolute explosive renaissance.  And we got the royalties and we got the ownership, and basically everybody sat on their fat butts and cashed in.

**EISNER:**  No, it's starting to happen, it's happening now.  But, really, this renaissance we're talking about was brought in by Neil Gaiman, Alan Moore, and people of that caliber, who are contributing vitally to the general intellectual configuration of the medium.

**MILLER:**  Sure, but one should pause to bellyache a little bit about the fact that no matter what efforts either of them have made, there's a vast number of people looking to do the same thing.

**EISNER:**  Of course.

**MILLER:**  I mean, I once did a cover of a Marvel comic, *Daredevil*, where I just drew a clichéd fat southern cop staring at the camera, saying, "We've got a nasty, rotten little town here, Mister, and we intend to keep it that way."  And to me, that was the comic book industry at the time *[laughs]*.

**EISNER:**  I am always completely amused when people refer to it as an "industry."  Or movies, calling movies an industry.  It's a profession; it's an art form.  To me, really, I am trying sell the idea that there's very little difference between us and the people who are writing books or any other form of literature.  We are a form of literature.

**MILLER:**  Sure, but we have an unusual amount of freedom that most people don't have.  I know a number of prose novelists who almost all have restrictions that you or I don't have, and they're more subject to marketing.  Like, it's much more important how they physically look, especially if they're female.  That's publishing.

In comics we have this strange view that we're a separate world, and we aren't. We're part of an evolving, changing industry.

**EISNER:** One of the points I think you're trying to make is that there's a big difference between the guys working in the field today and when you started. Then, you were trapped by the publishers themselves. They owned everything. If you tried to start a publishing company at that time, you had to have enough money to be able to go into the business, for one thing. You had to have enough money to be able to back up a distribution contract. And at that point, you wouldn't give a royalty to anybody; you'd want to own the property. That was the difference. The publisher had complete control, and he exerted it by telling you, the writer and author, and the artist, "We can replace you."

> **"We're talking about an art form that had a very stunted, strange development, but it's just getting started."**

**MILLER:** The perfect physical prop I recall is that they always had a fill-in issue in a flat file, in case you were late. Because they didn't have late books. You'd be fired [for being late]. And that way they had absolute control. Now, I gotta say, I regard that as legitimate, because they're publishing periodicals and they've gotta deliver on time. But there was something about the way they'd point to that damn drawer, and you'd know that you were just another person who came through those doors. There were very few people back then who could be called stars in the field. And mostly it was just, "Okay, he's the guy on *Dr. Strange.*"

**EISNER:** I guess you can compare it to a football team or baseball team. "He's a good player, so therefore we're going to take care of him. We'll keep him around, because he's good at what he's doing." If you were better than anybody else, that's what kept you there. If you could draw better, you could do *Superman* better than the other guy did …

**MILLER:** You had to be obedient.

**EISNER:** Well, of course. If you made trouble, you would talk yourself out of business.

> **"In comics we have this strange view that we're a separate world, and we aren't. We're part of an evolving, changing industry."**

**MILLER:** For instance, there was always a whisper campaign against Neal Adams. I'm not talking out of school here; everybody knew about it. Neal certainly knew about it. But there was always a murmuring campaign about how he wasn't "professional" and he "didn't like to work." How he was a troublemaker. He's the hardest-working guy I ever met. He just wanted his original artwork back.

**EISNER:** The word you're talking about, "troublemaker," that's the one that I remember.

**MILLER:** In the world of comic books, "troublemaker" means someone who has some sense of dignity. The whole way people are judged — by how many pages they produce per week and how many books per month …

**EISNER:** If you're the manager of a football team, you want to know how many yards you're going to gain, rushing in a season. If a guy's a

**Miller lampoons the notion of being a "team player"** in this scene from *Sin City: Hell and Back #1*. © *1999 Frank Miller, Inc.*

troublemaker, it's because he's talking to the other football players and saying, "We've gotta organize to get a better deal."

**MILLER:** If you have a choice between getting a hundred pages by John Buscema that are magnificent or five hundred that he crapped out, I'd rather have the hundred. And the whole [business] was set up to make people like John Buscema into nothing more than production machines.

> "In the world of comic books, 'troublemaker' means someone who has some sense of dignity."

**EISNER:** The trouble with you, Frank, is that you're thinking like a 21st-century man. You're not thinking like a guy in the thirties or forties. If you were thinking like a guy in the forties, you'd say you wanted comic books that were "good enough" for what you needed to sell. It was a buyer's market. They regarded each guy the way they would regard an athlete. And, sure, you knock yourself out to keep a good athlete who's got a batting average over 400, but you're not going to give him the right to own a percentage of the club because of that. You know that sooner or later he's going to give out, or sooner or later you will have to replace him. So I think the big difference in the attitude of publishers towards cartoonists working in the field today is essentially that they're buying *people.* They're buying Frank Miller; they're buying names. They're not necessarily buying the character itself. And that's a big change.

**MILLER:** It's kind of a mixed bag these days, because there is the religiously devoted audience that really does care more about Green Lantern.

**EISNER:** Do you mean there's a group of people who really care more about Batman himself, rather than Frank Miller's version of Batman?

**MILLER:** Absolutely, and they hate my guts!

**EISNER:** Really? I find it hard to believe that.

**MILLER:** Yeah. I'm really honking off the "religious" ones these days because I'm trammeling all over these characters. They think it's hallowed ground, and I think it's a fun toy.

**EISNER:** Well. I never worked in that system. I didn't have to. Start with that: I didn't *have* to do that.

**MILLER:** Well, the newspaper section was a masterstroke.

**EISNER:** It was a very opportune thing, and there was no competition to speak of. I was moving in the area that I wanted to move. I wanted to write to adults. Anyway, any time I'd draw a superhero, he'd look like he was made out of foam rubber.

**MILLER:** One of the things I really do love about the Spirit is how goofy his mask actually looks. It didn't fit all that well.

**EISNER:** It's an absurd premise anyway: a guy walking around in a mask and gloves, and nobody says anything. That's a reason I never liked superheroes. And I couldn't see myself getting into any one of the major houses in the fifties, or mid-fifties, doing comics. I had done that; there was no future. Remember, by then I was obsessed with the idea that there was a place to go with this medium, and at that time I believed almost romantically that there was a big opening in the instructional field for this medium to go into. I proved the point while I was in the army, and I fought against the army establishment to use comics as a teaching tool. There was a big struggle, because the Adjutant General wanted to kill *P.S.* [Eisner's instructional army manual, done in comics form]. They even attempted to discontinue it by running a test at the University of Chicago; they ran a test between my comic and a technical manual, and we beat the hell out of them.  We got a readership that they never would get.  So I didn't have to yield at that time.  I didn't want to.  If my company had collapsed at that time and I'd had nothing and was on the street, I still doubt whether I would have gone back into the comic book field, because it offered no future to me.  I had already done that.

**MILLER:**  The point I keep returning to so often here, though, is that it was strange to enter a field where everyone was so unhappy but the material itself was so joyful — brightly colored characters, insane universes, and all that.  Coming in, young kids like me loved what we were doing, but there was a sense that by the time we turned fifty we were gonna be miserable.  People seemed to get so bitter so young.

**EISNER:**  You saw that in the guys around you, when you went into the office and saw the old cartoonists?  I was never a fellow cartoonist, unfortunately, so I was never able to get the kind of remarks that you might have gotten sitting down and having a beer.  So, I don't know, maybe there was that atmosphere when you got in.  Was there?

**MILLER:**  Well, there wasn't much contact between generations, but the older guys were generally known as a fairly bitter bunch.

**Miller sees corporate characters as "fun toys" — not as grounds for religious reverence.  From *DK2* volume 3.  © *2002 DC Comics***

**EISNER:** Oh, really?

**MILLER:** Yeah. And when you tried to get John Buscema, when he was around, to talk about his craft, he'd speak in the most disparaging terms. The guy drew like Michelangelo. He talked like a truck driver. I wrote one story that he drew, and he loved it because there was nobody in tights. *[Eisner laughs.]*

*[Miller gruffly imitates Buscema.]* "I keep drawing these frigging superheroes all the time." He liked Conan because Conan killed people! But there was this sense of ... "We're just workaday Joes. Don't stand too tall. Don't talk too proud."

**EISNER:** Ah, that's interesting.

**MILLER:** That's why Neal Adams was such a dramatic figure.

**EISNER:** He stood tall, and he talked proud. Again, Neal Adams proved he didn't need the comic book industry. He went into advertising.

**MILLER:** And we lost a lot of his comics with him doing that, which is too bad, you know? We lost a lot of your comics, too, for that matter.

**EISNER:** But I came back on a different platform. Had I stayed in the field, I don't know whether I would have lasted. When *The Spirit* hit the newsstands in competition with the comic books, it never did well. I wasn't talking to the fans.

**MILLER:** Well, it brought new ideas. And I can't speak for Neal, but I don't think he'd disagree that what is different between you two is that Neal doesn't have any real quarrel with the content of comics as superhero comics. He likes them. When he published his own comics line, it was very much in the same vein. *You* were challenging the content and the architecture.

**Eisner was forced to give the Spirit a mask as a means of satisfying his publisher's demand for a "costumed" character. This illustration was taken from the back cover of** *The Spirit Coloring Book.* © *1974 Will Eisner*

**EISNER:** All right. Yes, I was. But they hadn't really matured. There was a whole area that they could go to, there was a whole market of readers that they could go to, but that they hadn't gone to.

**MILLER:** This is tangential, but part of the function of maturity is that at some point you decide you're not a rebel anymore. I realized at one point that if I have a relationship with DC Comics or Marvel Comics, it's one of mutual interest to me.  It can't be me rebelling against them.  And I've got the clout now where I can come in and wreak havoc on their old mythologies, but I'm not rebelling.

**EISNER:**  A lot of where we thought we were rebels at the beginning … we realize now that the medium has distinct segments.  It has separate jobs.  The writer's job, the penciller's job, the inker's job, the letterer's job, the publisher's job, they're all part of this whole big thing, and they can't, any of them, live without the other.

**MILLER:**  Yeah, but I think we do have to look at the infrastructure with new eyes in order to figure out how to survive, because right now it's not working.  We have a larger audience than we're accessing; we simply do.  I've given away so many free copies of my books to people, and then they ask, "Where can I find it?"  And I have to direct them to some comics shop that's halfway across town, and I can see in their eyes they'll never bother.

**EISNER:**  I agree, we haven't yet gotten the audience that we seek.

**MILLER:**  I don't think we're even close to it.  At the same time, I don't think we have an audience in the multimillions, but I think it's in the multithousands.  I think there are hundreds of thousands of potential casual readers, and I want those other thousands.

# 18.......

# OLD TESTIMONY

*Eisner and Miller break for lunch at Sandtrap, a players' bar and grill at a golf course near the studio.*

**EISNER:** I'm being given a lifetime achievement award by the National Foundation for Jewish Culture.

**MILLER:** Cool! That's great!

**EISNER:** I've been hiding all these years, and now I'm coming out of the closet *[laughter]*.

**MILLER:** You heard it here first, folks: Will Eisner is Jewish.

**EISNER:** Well, actually, it was that impudent Jules Feiffer who outed me *[Miller laughs]*. He said, "The Spirit had an Irish name and a short nose, but we all knew he was Jewish."

..............................................................................................................

**Opposite: Cover art for the *Will Eisner Reader*. © 1991 Will Eisner**

**MILLER:**  It's about time Clark Kent came clean.  He's no Protestant.

**EISNER:**  No.  Let me see if I can put it this way: Arnold Toynbee wrote a book a long time ago about the heredity of culture.  The Jews, he said, were people who were on the run for 2,000 years, so those who remained who could survive in society have that heredity, an instinctive thing that stays with them over the years.  Then along came the Holocaust.  Now, Siegel and Shuster [the creators of Superman] were not attempting to answer the Holocaust on behalf of the Jewish people.  Siegel was a very simple guy, and he was writing a story that responded to the angst of the time. As a matter of fact, he sent me two stories at Eisner & Iger: one called "Spy" and the other called "Superman" — which I rejected.

**MILLER:**  Good call!

**EISNER:**  Yeah, great business judgment *[Miller laughs]*!  Well, actually, at the time the reason I rejected it was because we were not publishers; we were packagers, and I had reasoned that the guys we were selling packages to wouldn't buy it.

> **"Jerry Siegel sent me two stories at Eisner & Iger: one called 'Spy' and the other called 'Superman' — which I rejected."**

**MILLER:**  I do think the people who turned down *Superman* should have T-shirts that say so, just for laughs.

**EISNER:**  I think I would like to get an award or a plaque *[Miller laughs]*.  The point is that their idea was responsive to a subliminal

Jewish thought that is more universal than entirely Jewish. Remember, at that time, there was the Nazi force running through Europe. It appeared to be an irresistible force, and what you need to stop that force is an immovable object. The superhero they were creating was that immovable object. They didn't invent the idea; Edgar Rice Burroughs did it, the Bible did it …

**MILLER:** Yeah, it goes all the way back. Way before Batman, you had the Scarlet Pimpernel, you had Zorro. These characters have so many antecedents that none of them are wholly original.

> ## "There were Jews in this medium because it was a crap medium."

**EISNER:** What I'm trying to point out is that this whole business of the superhero is something that's been around all the time and is continually here. That's why superheroes will not disappear.

**MILLER:** I agree. The idea is all of sudden gaining steam again. It's losing relevance, but it's gaining steam. They'll be doing better superheroes in movies than they're doing in comics, before long.

**EISNER:** It was only accidental that Siegel and Shuster did what they did. However, if they'd been Irish, I think they still would have [created Superman], because it was a good idea. But you gotta think in terms of the fact that — and this has a little bit of mysticism to it — there is always, in a society, a kind of radiation that guides the thinking in that society.

**MILLER:** The Zeitgeist.

In a job market with racial overtones, many Jewish artists found it easier to get work in the "crap medium" of comics, rather than in the more prestigious field of magazine illustration. From *The Dreamer*. In actuality, "Lew Sharp" is, of course, artist Lou Fine. © *1986 Will Eisner*

..............................................................................................

**EISNER:** That's why superheroes became popular very quickly at that time. This country has always had superheroes.

**MILLER:** I guess the reason I jumped on this … there are two reasons. One is that all the creators of superheroes I'm aware of were Jewish; the second is that the stories are so loaded with Old Testament imagery. I mean, come on, the baby put in a rocket ship and sent across the sky …

**EISNER:** What I'm trying to say … the answer to your question, to your instinctive feeling, is yes. On the other hand, it was not conscious on the creators' part. They only wrote about the things that they felt or understood that might address the sense of the time. Jews grow up with the Bible, but so do Christians and Fundamentalists. But Jews for centuries have dealt with surviving persecution, and they look upon physical force as something they don't have.

I think you raise a very important question of why there were so many Jews in this medium. There were Jews in this medium because it was a crap medium. And in a marketplace that still had racial overtones, it was an easy medium to get into. There were only three or four Jews working in the daily [newspaper] strips; all the rest were Irish or something else. So you had two forces going along at the same time. First, you had a medium that was regarded as trash, that nobody really wanted to go into. Nobody who aspired to be a great illustrator regarded comics as more than crap. The second thing is that there was a group of people who could easily get into this business, and what they brought with them was their 2,000-year history of storytelling. These people were storytellers, because the only way they communicated the technique of survival to each other was by telling stories. They wrote the Bible.

# 19.......

# COWARDICE
# AND SHAME

**MILLER:** You've phrased all of this in business terms and I understand that, because it becomes clear when you get into the business thing that that's the arena you're in. But at various times you've obviously been involved in things of pretty big moment to the whole profession. Have you run into — as I have so often — naked, stupid cowardice on the part of a lot of people?

**EISNER:** *[Pause]* I'm going to think about that.

**MILLER:** I mean, the whole notion of "company loyalty" struck me as absurd from the first day.

........................................................................

**Opposite: During his years in the field, Miller claims to have often encountered naked cowardice on the part of both publishers and artists. From *Sin City: That Yellow Bastard #3.* © 1996 Frank Miller, Inc.**

**EISNER:** Since I have never really worked for a company … now is the first time that I've worked *with* — not for, but with — a major company. It's the first time I've ever come across that. But as far as company loyalty is concerned, you're absolutely right. I know that, early on, there actually was such a thing as company loyalty.

**MILLER:** Company loyalty is the battered wife's excuse.

**EISNER:** The company now has no loyalty to you, and you have no loyalty to it. But the loyalty is generally to the person above you, and you count on getting a certain amount of loyalty to them.

> ### "Company loyalty is the battered wife's excuse."

**MILLER:** I have loyalty to people, but how can you have loyalty to a *company* when it's made of people and they're interchangeable?

**EISNER:** Loyalties develop between an editor and a following. Editors get jobs because they have a following. I'm talking about major publishing houses. If you have an editor who's got, say, Arthur Miller as one of his authors and he goes with his editor to whatever new publisher, that's something that has some value, and that's a relationship.

**MILLER:** Yeah, a good editor is irreplaceable.

**EISNER:** But I'm trying to think of it. You asked me a very good question, and I don't know if I've run into any real naked cowardice on the part of any one artist.

**MILLER:** How about during the fifties, during the troubles with the Kefauver Hearings? Were people denying what they did for a living?

**EISNER:** A lot of people did. A lot of artists would not come into the field.

**MILLER:** I heard that Bernie Krigstein denied he ever did comics.

**EISNER:** I never met Bernie Krigstein, but I heard he was a kind of stormy guy. He had firm visions and strong ideas and knew what he wanted to do. He quit the business after a while. I was told he quit the business because he couldn't make a living. He felt there was not enough money in it, they said. The only so-called cowardice I ever heard about was Kirby's unwillingness to break loose from one of the major companies. He was perfectly willing to go from DC to Marvel and back and forth between the two, but beyond that he would not go.[1] Is that what you call cowardice?

**MILLER:** No. I was thinking there were people who just definitely wouldn't show up when it was time to stand as a group about something.

**EISNER:** I was never involved in that. Did you ever run into something like that?

**MILLER:** Oh, yeah, especially during that rather stormy period when Neal Adams raised hell and inspired a contentious bunch of artists, myself included …

**EISNER:** Was there an attempt to start a group?

**MILLER:** Well, Neal Adams attempted the [Artists'] Guild, and, while that effort failed, it was almost like it planted the seed that made historic success, because it changed the way we all talked and thought.

**EISNER:** Why did the thing fail?

...........................................................................................

[1] Until the 1981 release of Kirby's *Captain Victory*, published by the now-defunct Pacific Comics.

**MILLER:** Because it needed to have the big hands. The more productive artists needed to be involved in order to give it any power. That's how I understand it. I was not in all the meetings. I was really a beginner at the time. But a lot of the more productive people at Marvel and DC wouldn't join it because they were afraid to lose their jobs.

**EISNER:** Well, see, yeah. Something like that you can't …

**MILLER:** Another case involves [former DC Comics publisher] Jenette Kahn. DC was making a rather bold move to raid the talent at Marvel. Jenette Kahn had been there a few years, was at the top of her game, and introduced, basically, a royalty system. It wasn't called that, because they didn't want to concede the intellectual point! But it was a royalty system. When this was announced, Marvel didn't know what to do at first, and there was a very tense stretch of three or four days when nobody really knew what Marvel was gonna do. And I came in to the Marvel offices to tell them that they had to do something about this.

**EISNER:** Or what? Or you would leave?

**MILLER:** Yes.

**EISNER:** Were you prepared to follow that up?

So much for "union solidarity"! From *The Dreamer*. © *1986 Will Eisner*

**MILLER:** Yes. What happened was, I went in and the office door was closed, and a message had come in from another artist who'd said, "Don't worry, I'll stay with you [Marvel] no matter what you do." So I just took a piece of notepaper and wrote, "Match it or I walk." I taped that to the door and left.

I've seen plenty of times when people were losing work, and I've certainly heard a number of my colleagues mention the fact that they have kids, because that's the excuse that everybody uses for any act of cowardice.

**EISNER:** The only time I was involved in something like that was very early on in '37 or '38 when Bob Kane brought me down to a union meeting. A union of cartoonists. These were panel cartoonists, doing single panels for *Liberty Magazine* and *College Humor* — that was a big market at the time for cartoonists. This was before comic books. And he said that there was a cartoonists' union being started. So I went to the union meeting, and they made a resolution that they would not sell a single panel for less than seven dollars a panel. They were getting five dollars a panel. Well, the thing collapsed about three weeks later when a bunch of guys quit and another bunch of guys went to the same editors and said, "Okay, I'll sell it for five dollars." They were never able to control their union.

**MILLER:** In the interest of full disclosure, I've got to admit I came down on the wrong side of the Guild effort, because my father was a rabid anti-union guy. And also, I felt myself fortunate that I'd just gotten a job at Marvel Comics, so I was not a part of that effort. I ran some errands for the Guild, but I did sign Marvel's new "voucher" form that just happened to insist that Marvel owned everything forever. It was that form that inspired Neal to try to start the Guild. Marvel had turned its billing format into a unilateral contract, and I was young and stupid, so I signed it. We all did.

**EISNER:** You got a job doing artwork?

**MILLER:** I was drawing comics, yeah.

**EISNER:** What did they give you at the time? Did they give you a page rate? Did they guarantee you any quantity of work?

**MILLER:** I got a page rate. I started at DC at $25 a page for pencils, and eventually at Marvel I was getting $30-$35 a page, and was becoming proficient enough and the boss was liking my stuff enough that he guaranteed me regular work, and I was never without it after that.

> ### "The reason I got involved in certain scuffles was self-interest."

**EISNER:** See, it was a different kind of thing. It was a question of guaranteed work …

**MILLER:** The thing is, I've got to say I didn't come in feeling at all like a big gun. The reason I got involved in certain scuffles was self-interest. It made sense, and it also gave me the sense that all this work amounts to something. To me, issues of royalties were essentially tied into what you'd established with *A Contract with God*. To having annuities. To having longstanding —

**EISNER:** Properties. You were building equity. The only equity any cartoonist had in those days was his ability to produce and be regarded by the house as a competent producer. That was the equity he built. And that was misunderstood as loyalty. They thought of it as loyalty.

**MILLER:** The weird thing, though — and this is another thing I wonder about the careers of comic book artists — is I was lucky, in that I did a regular monthly comic book in the trenches for four or five years.

Whatever it was, it was about a year too long, because my last year's work wasn't very good. I'd lost interest, and I wasn't admitting it to myself because I had gotten pretty comfortable and the book was very popular. But I saw so many people who'd been doing the same comic book month after month for decade after decade, and I don't see how one could really do that without just eventually burning out completely on it.

**EISNER:** It's amazing, but daily strip cartoonists do it year in and year out. At one time, like all cartoonists, I thought having a daily strip would be the most wonderful thing in the world. The problem with that, I discovered later, is you have to be the same guy you were when you started at the newspaper. Clients expect you to be what you were when they bought you in the first place, so for the next fifty years you have to do the same thing!

**MILLER:** That's the nature of clients.

**EISNER:** It's the nature of the business ... the market.

> "The only equity any cartoonist had in those days was his ability to produce and be regarded by the house as a competent producer."

**MILLER:** Whenever I revisit something, people wonder why it's not the same as it was last time. And when it comes to something like the first *Dark Knight* series and then doing a sequel fifteen years later, people say, "It's not right." And I say, "You're not fifteen anymore."

**EISNER:** That's right.

**MILLER:** I wouldn't go back and do something the same way. That's like dying.

**EISNER:** But, you see, for the daily strip cartoonists it's the same thing for year after year after year. Look at *Peanuts*.

**MILLER:** That went through quite an evolution for a strip.

**EISNER:** It didn't change very much from the first ones he [Charles Schulz] did.

**MILLER:** The drawing changed.

**EISNER:** Not that much. It improved a little bit, but not that much. For example, when I did the daily *Spirit* strip, one of the big problems I had was experimentation. I did a *Spirit* strip one day that was just footsteps in the snow. I got such a blast, from the syndicate; they called me up in a dead panic and said, "We're going to get cancellations if you keep doing something like that. We're going to lose papers!"

**MILLER:** I've always been amazed that the hierarchy among cartoonists seems to be that you're lower on the rank with the more panels you do *[laughter]*. There's a four-panel barrier: if you go beyond four, then all of a sudden it's "juvenile." The editorial cartoonists don't fall over the strip guys, and the strip guys don't fall over us. Everybody knows it.

**Eisner's experimentation in *The Spirit* daily strip was frowned upon by the Register and Tribune Syndicate.** *© 1942 Will Eisner*

**EISNER:** The daily strip cartoonist was the aristocracy for a long time. They still are, in many ways.

**MILLER:** Although I think that Bill Watterson gave them a kick in the pants. Have you seen that one *Calvin and Hobbes* episode where it's all the same panel and Calvin is talking about how lazy cartoonists are to use Xeroxes in their strips *[laughter]*?

> "I've always been amazed that
> the hierarchy among cartoonists
> seems to be that you're lower
> on the rank with the more panels
> you do. There's a four-panel barrier:
> if you go beyond four, then all of
> a sudden it's 'juvenile.'"

**EISNER:** I never saw that. He was marvelous.

**MILLER:** He was vociferous in his attacks. Why [aspire to] the newspapers? All the strips are too small, and they're not worth it anyway.

**EISNER:** Well, the saddest moment I had … I think I covered it in my *Shop Talk* interview with Milton Caniff. We were discussing the same thing. He pulled out a couple photocopies of his daily strips, and he said, "Look at this. They're getting smaller and smaller, and I can no longer do the artwork I used to do." He was very sad. He was very unhappy about it. To this day you open up a page, and there's a whole *stack* of strips.

**MILLER:** It's almost a mercy that the *New York Times* doesn't run comics.

Says Eisner, Lynn Johnston's *For Better or For Worse* has all the characteristics of a good strip: "It's humane, human, it has humor to it, and good artwork."
© *1999 Lynn Johnston Productions, Inc.*

**EISNER:** Their idea of comics is primitive art.

**MILLER:** Bill Wiley does good stuff. Jerry Scott and Ken Gordon do a really nicely drawn, fun, cartoony strip called *Zits*. And the *Boondocks* strip is a highlight because it's got some life in it. But after that it gets really thin.

**EISNER:** Here goes an endorsement that's going to make trouble for me, but my idea of the best strip around currently is Lynn Johnston's *For Better or For Worse*. It has all the characteristics of what I consider a good strip. It's humane, human, it has humor to it, and good artwork.

**MILLER:** The characters age, and they have a lot of personality.

**EISNER:** The only one that ever tried that, early on, was *Gasoline Alley*, where the characters all grew up. But strips today … the strips are ganged up on a page.

**MILLER:** Watterson campaigned to make Sunday pages the size they ought to be. Finally, they started running his strip bigger.

**EISNER:** He was sensationally brilliant. His idea was not a new idea, but the way it was executed was amazing.

**MILLER:** To me, looking at the future of comic strips is kind of like asking about the future of the nickelodeon or something.

**EISNER:** I don't know how much of a future they have. I got into a discussion one day with Mort Walker [creator of *Beetle Bailey*], and he disagreed with me, but I said, "Mort, if any newspaper today decided to cancel all its comic strips, I don't think they'd lose a bit of circulation." "You're dead wrong," he said, "they'd be murdered." But if there's no other paper in town … I ran a newspaper syndicate, Bell McClure, for a short time. My salesmen could go call on a paper in a town and say to the editor, "I've got a comic strip here, and if you don't buy it I'll offer it to your competitor." That ploy lasted only until we began to find that most major cities were "one-paper towns." When I left the syndicate field, the opportunities for new strips were diminishing. Newspapers no longer believe that comic strips deliver circulation like they did in the competitive era of the twenties and thirties.

# 20......
# BITTERNESS
# AND BACKSTABBING

**MILLER:** Let's get back into the culture of the early comics business. [Harry] Donenfeld had this "property" attitude, you said. How did this evolve? How did it go from "We've gotta keep these presses running" to this intellectual property greed?

**EISNER:** First of all, the properties they had were not regarded as *intellectual*! Later, we earned the term "intellectual" in here *[laughs]*.

**MILLER:** So, before us, the legal term was "moronic property" *[laughter]*.

**EISNER:** "Idiot property"! No, they were properties. Just property. Bob Kane brings the publishers Batman; from then on, they own Batman. It's their property. Remember that no superhero created before

1960 is being done today by the guy who originated it. Every one of those characters has been done by other people along the way, and they built an ambiance around the character that far exceeds what the creator had originally done. Batman was originated by Bob Kane — a simple man and a very simple character — and along came Jerry Robinson who added dimension, solid artwork to it. Later, along came Frank Miller, who added a dimension of intellect and emotion. That's what's been happening. So the change that has taken place over the years has been the implantation, if you will, of an internal kind of growth.

## "The motivation is always desperation."

**MILLER:** Here again, Will, that's a very pretty way of putting it, but beneath that, how much backstabbing was actually going on? There are a lot of bitter voices from those days.

**EISNER:** I think of backstabbing as cheating another guy or shoving another guy out. Perhaps there was a lot of that; I don't know. Remember, the guys who had control of things were the guys who had control of the "property." Donenfeld, or [Jack] Liebowitz, who was his *consigliere,* or, later on, the editors who were running the thing … they were in control of giving work to people. They were the ones who assigned somebody to a character. Somebody had to make a decision and say, "Yeah, let's let Frank Miller do *Batman.*" A very courageous thing at the time, considering what *Batman* did for them.

**MILLER:** No, they were desperate. The book was in the toilet.

**EISNER:** Frank, the motivation is always desperation *[laughs].*

**MILLER:** They didn't need to reach for it.

**EISNER:** The backstabbing that you're talking about was the name of the game in business. If you were working for a comic book house and you didn't own the property that you were working on, then you had to be nice to the editor. Your fate was in the hands of an editor who was assigning work. When I was running American Visuals, my art director was in charge of giving freelance work out to guys in the shop — overtime work and so forth, which was *extra money*. He was in total control. He was "the man." They had to be nice to him. You had to be nice to [former publisher Carmine] Infantino or [former production manager] Sol Brodsky in order to get enough work out of DC. If you were a tough guy to deal with, you wouldn't get any work. There was competition for work. But since you didn't own the property, it was an unstable playing field. It comes right down to piecework. But once you own the property …

**MILLER:** That I understand, but, still, what we're talking about is a really bloody goddamn history. I remember when they were announcing the fiftieth anniversary of Superman, I was sick over the celebration because I was thinking, "I've met a lot of these guys. There's an awful lot of ill will; there are an awful lot of ruined lives."

> "The backstabbing that you're talking about was the name of the game in business."

You're one of the success stories, Will, but there are an awful lot of your compadres who ended up pretty damn bitter. Kirby was gonna write a book called *Excelsior, My Ass!*

**EISNER:** Jack was bitter, and I understand why Jack was bitter. He felt that Stan [Lee] got too much credit for creation. There were other guys who, I suppose, were bitter. Gil Kane was angry. Very curious — brilliant guy, but he seemed to be swimming upstream.

**Publishers alternative to Marvel and DC began to spring up in the late seventies, finally allowing comics creators the opportunity to own their own work. Although published by Dark Horse, all the rights to *Sin City* are owned by its creator. From *Sin City: That Yellow Bastard* #2. © *1996 Frank Miller, Inc.***

**MILLER:** He was a guy who was able to intellectualize what Kirby did instinctively and create a formula around it to make a very dynamic page, but with all his brains he just kept drawing stupid stories.

**EISNER:** He couldn't break out, largely because, like most creators, nobody in the field — *no one* — ever took a chance or attempted to own their own thing.

**MILLER:** You kept *The Spirit*.

**EISNER:** Yeah, but I was willing to pay for it; I walked away without work. A lot of guys weren't willing to pay [that price]. Joe Simon told me that he turned to Jack Kirby at one point and said, "Jack, let's break away from these guys and go out on our own." And Jack said, "Oh, no —

I'll never get any work from these guys again." It's like the movie business: "You'll never work in this town again."

**MILLER:** That's exactly when you leave the room. Because you've lost everything.

**EISNER:** You've gotta be willing to pay the price to do something like that. Look, I don't blame them; it's a very hard thing to do. If your total income is coming from Marvel or DC or one of the major companies, and it comes from the amount of pencilling work that you're going to get next week and the amount and quality of scripts they're going to give you, by then you're not a *name* anymore. Yes, if you're a Frank Miller or a Neil Gaiman or a Neal Adams, you can walk in there and say you want to get a certain amount of work, and you'll get it.

> ## "Jack Kirby was gonna write a book called *Excelsior, My Ass!*"

**MILLER:** But these *names* are not dropped from heaven upon us. It's because people like you were willing to "leave the room" — that's one of the reasons why we *have* "names." I was exclusive to one publisher for at least two years — Marvel Comics. I worked exclusively for them and had a monthly quota of the number of pages I would deliver. I was not quite guaranteed work, but promised enough work to fill that quota. For me, that was a wonderful breakthrough in my life, to have a predictable income very early in my career. But Neal Adams had already planted the seed; you'd done *A Contract with God.* Various explosions were happening in my brain, and I honestly at one point realized that the whole notion of exclusivity contracts was absurd, because I was throwing away my only real bargaining chip.

**EISNER:** See, now, on the other side of that coin, at one time, early on, I would have loved to have had a guaranteed contract like the one you had.

**The death of the pulp market, as told by Eisner in *The Dreamer*.**
© *1986 Will Eisner*

**MILLER:**   But I have found that working with different publishers always makes the homecoming more welcome!

**EISNER:**   *[Laughs]* That's so true.   Absence makes the heart grow fonder.   Or abstinence!   You had to start somewhere, Frank, but you also established a value in yourself, and that brings us back to what you were searching for.   The word "backstabbing," to me, means one cartoonist, one artist, trying to cut the throat of or undercut another cartoonist.   I don't think that is what was really happening, simply because cartoonists didn't have the muscle.   What was really happening was that, up until the seventies, the publishers had total control because there was no other market.   There was no choice for a Jeff Smith or a Dave Sim or Wendy Pini [artists who became self-publishers].   There was no alternative.   You couldn't take a couple hundred dollars, go off and find an offset press, do a thousand copies and distribute them, and then start growing from there.

> **"I have found that working with different publishers always makes the homecoming more welcome!"**

Everything you think about those times has gotta be factored within the frame of the total picture.   Publishers had distribution control.   When I started at Eisner & Iger, I reasoned there was a marketplace, because the major pulp publishers were losing their market. The pulp market was dying.   But the pulp publishers had something — they had distribution contracts with the American News Company, and those were valuable things, so they were looking for things to publish that were like pulps.   And that's how the comic book marketplace got under way.   In order to get a comic book printed in 1938 or '39, you had to print three to five hundred thousand copies!   The distributor said, "You've gotta give us three hundred thousand copies before we'll even touch this." And they said, "We can return as many as we can't sell." So you had to be strong enough to be able to withstand the return of maybe a hundred thousand or two hundred and fifty thousand copies. If you had a fifty percent sale, you were making money, you were riding high. Magazines were costing you two to three cents a copy, and you were selling them to a news company for five cents a copy, so you were making something like a hundred percent markup or a seventy percent markup, and you could afford a thirty percent return. The thing changed with the [change in] distribution. When distribution was altered, by Phil Seuling, into a comic book specialty market,[1] what he did was provide publishers with a floor, so they could go ahead and take a chance on a new Frank Miller or a new Will Eisner or a new whoever, taking pre-publication orders so they wouldn't get hurt [by returns]. Whereas a major publishing house that used to sell on newsstands, with the possibility of having returns dumped on their doorstep in thirty days, couldn't take a chance on anything that didn't have a record of sure sales. So, think of that.

**MILLER:** Sure, but how was the system built back when you started? What was it like for you coming into this field, dealing with mobsters, dealing with the corruption of the publishing business, and having this passion for the art form that you had to convey within this strange business structure?

**EISNER:** It was tough. The conditions were … you had an idea and you had to give it away — literally — to a publisher, in exchange for a promise of work. I was at Bob Kane's house when he came back with the contract that he'd just got for Batman. His father was an insurance man, and he brought his father down to negotiate with Donenfeld's man. What they were told was, "We own this property. It's ours. But what we will give you is a promise of work." That's all he got: a promise of work. He got so much per page and a promise of work as long as he wanted to do work on the feature. But they owned the property.

......................................................................................

[1] Also known as the "direct market."

**MILLER:** I — and a lot of other people, I think — assumed that he'd gotten a much better arrangement.

**EISNER:** No, not at first he didn't. That happened later. Bob was a very lucky man. He was at a cocktail party when a lawyer came up to him and said, "Hey, Bob, do you own Batman?" He said, "No, not really." And the lawyer asked to see his contract. So Bob showed it to him, and the lawyer then had a bright idea, went up to DC, and said to them, "Look, you're about to make a movie …" Remember the first campy television movie? They were negotiating with television to make a Batman movie. And DC said to him, "You don't have a case." And he said, "I may not have a case, but I'm going to cost you that movie, so let's make a deal." They made a deal.

**MILLER:** So that was the precedent for Siegel and Shuster.

**EISNER:** No, the Siegel and Shuster thing was something else again. That was something organized by Jerry Robinson and Neal Adams [in 1975] to embarrass Warner Brothers into giving Siegel and Shuster some kind of sinecure. A whole gang of us got together and kept talking to the Associated Press. We made a big stink. We talked to the AP, and they said, "Oh, boy, this is a good story," and they began releasing stories on it. So DC said, "Hey, wait a minute, hold it!"

**MILLER:** You've got a blind postal worker who co-created Superman — the press was all over that!

**EISNER:** Well, Frank, there are two sides to that coin. Remember that, in 1935, when Siegel and Shuster sold Superman, first of all, nobody would buy it. Secondly, no one thought it was worth anything. Third, when they got it, they had no contract; what they got was a check, a *regular* check, and back then, during the Depression, a regular *anything* was good! The back of the check read: "For all rights and title." So when they signed the check to get it cashed, they had signed away the rights. Later on, some smart lawyer was able to get a judge to say that wasn't a real contract.

The infamous back-of-the-check contract:
by endorsing their paychecks, artists
were made to sign away any claim to their
own work. **From** *The Dreamer.*
© *1986 Will Eisner*

...................................................

**MILLER:** Boy, that was a real shock wave, too, because I'd signed dozens of them and it'd been modified just enough so that the publisher would own everything forever. Not just the rights to the work you were selling, but to *all* your work for them. Anyway, Neal Adams just hoisted a Jolly Roger. He had Xeroxed these posters everywhere that said, "Don't sign this! You're signing your life away!" And that was when he tried to start the Guild. He must have talked to you about that.

**EISNER:** I know; he did try that. The Guild didn't work. He did scare the daylights out of these people. The field owes a lot to Neal for doing something like that, but ...

**MILLER:** He also changed the way a lot of us thought.

**EISNER:** Look, after starting Eisner & Iger, I no longer felt like I was trapped in this marketplace. I could start my own company; I could go somewhere. Most of the guys in the field had no choice; there was no place they could go. Bob Kane couldn't go anywhere; he had to take the contract that they gave him. He lucked out, as I said. In the fifties, his lawyer got him a new deal, but he still didn't own the property. They agreed to give him a sinecure of fifty thousand dollars a year and one percent of their merchandise income. Which turned out to be a lot of money. It turned out to be a million bucks or more, but at the time it was nothing. They were getting five percent from the toy manufacturer, and one percent of *that* was very little. But the important thing for Bob Kane was … Bob had a different agenda. He needed the ego stroking. Fifty thousand dollars a year for twenty years is a million dollars. Also, it was very lucky for him that the [Batman] movies did so well and that the staff DC assembled continued the comic book so successfully.

Let me ask you, though, what was the choice of a young cartoonist in 1950 going up to Marvel or DC with his black portfolio? When they say, "Okay, that's a great idea, we'll take it and we own it," and he says, "No, I want to own it," and they tell him to forget it. What choice did he have?

**MILLER:** The same choice we had in 1976 — which was *none*.

**EISNER:** But, in 1976, you had a choice. You could put a few bucks together and self-publish.

> "If there was any life left in the industry, I thought this must be it: self-publishing is the way it's going to go."

**MILLER:** A couple years later you could; I don't know if you could have then.

**EISNER:** You're right: in 1976 there weren't enough stores yet. Three or four years later, you could go somewhere else.

**MILLER:** Yeah, and Denis Kitchen was around [by then].

**Denis Kitchen (in the background) and Will Eisner, caricatured by the respective artists themselves. From the Kitchen Sink *Spirit* #22. © 1979 Will Eisner and Denis Kitchen**

**EISNER:** I met Denis in 1972 at an early Seuling convention,[2] and he had his Krupp Comics started by then. He had his own shop, and he was publishing comic books. In those days, the guys on the west coast were publishing their own comic books and selling them themselves.[3] Whatever [Robert] Crumb was doing, he was selling enough comics, I guess. So there was an alternative. Maybe before that, there was no alternative. Also, the technology wasn't there. You had offset presses that came in during the sixties, small offset presses. You could print a thousand copies on a small offset press and sell them to comic book shops. When I was teaching school, I used to encourage a lot of the students to do that.

For me, 1972 was a turning point. That was the year I was encouraged to come back into the field. I had a choice of which way I was going to go, and if there was any life left in the industry, I thought this must be it: self-publishing is the way it's going to go. To me the turning point was discovering the undergrounds and Phil Seuling's invitation to his convention.

**MILLER:** Phil Seuling did profoundly change things.

[2] During the seventies, Phil Seuling held a Fourth of July comics convention every year in New York City — a precursor to today's type of comics convention.

[3] Kitchen's company, unlike many underground comics publishers, was actually based in Wisconsin (until 1993).

**EISNER:** Oh, it was a shock to me. I was a "suit" at the time. I was the CEO of a publishing company selling to schools, and my secretary came in — this nice, blue-haired lady from up in New England — and she said, "Mr. Eisner, there's a call for you. A fellow named Phil Seuling. Do you know him?" I said no, and she said, "Well, he's got a comic magazine convention in New York, and he says he'd like you to come down to the show." She could hardly say the words; she whispered, "Were you a cartoonist at one time?" I said yeah. "Oh," she said, and handed me the phone. It was Seuling. Yes, I said I'd come to his show. And to my astonishment, guys were walking around carrying copies of the comic that I had shut down twenty years before! It was 1952 when I cut *The Spirit* out completely, and here it was 1972 and these little fat kids with pimply faces and their bellies sticking out and glasses that looked like the bottom of Coke bottles … these kids were carrying my comics around. And there was, of course, Denis Kitchen and Art Spiegelman and Spain Rodriguez and all these underground hippies with long hair and glassy eyes and a faint funny smell around them!

**MILLER:** *[Laughing]* You've learned since what that was, haven't you, Will?

**EISNER:** I didn't know at the time!

But I knew there was a change, and something was happening. That was very exciting to me. I left the convention, and a very fortunate thing happened. Somebody came along and asked if my company was for sale — so I said yeah and got out.

# 21.....

# THE SCHEMER

**MILLER:** You have what seem to be separate but almost equal passions for art and commerce.

**EISNER:** I love business.

**MILLER:** I've run into this myself. I love doing comic books, but it's ultimately lonely work and it does reach the point where you've been alone with it for too long. That's when I want to mix it up with other people, and I do it through business. There's a sense of accomplishing something in the three-dimensional world.

**EISNER:** To me business is a game — and I love the game, and I think I'm good at it.

.........................................................................................

**Opposite: Will Eisner circa 1960: the dreamer *and* the schemer.** *Photo courtesy of Denis Kitchen.*

**Eisner's father was a dreamer, whereas his mother was more pragmatic. From *The Dreamer*. © 1986 Will Eisner**

**MILLER:** In talking to you, I do get a sense that there's the dreamer and then there's the *schemer*! And they're two separate people.

**EISNER:** Oh, yeah.

**MILLER:** I want to read *The Schemer*!

**EISNER:** I haven't done that yet. That's a great book title, *The Schemer*! No, as a matter of fact, an old friend of mine, a psychiatrist, knew something about my family life. My mother was a more pragmatic person; my father was a dreamer. And my friend said, "What you're trying to do is please both your mother *and* your father. When you're sitting behind this desk you're pleasing your mother, and over at your drawing table you're pleasing your father." And it's true in a way, because my mother used to say to me, "You're never going to make any money out of this. Your father was starving to death trying to be an artist, and he could never make a living at it. Your uncle Louie *did* starve to death being an artist. What are you going to do with yourself? Why don't you do something legitimate, like being a teacher or something like that? Get a job!" I enjoy the business side. I understand and love the game.

**MILLER:** I do okay with business. I think what I enjoy most about business is its political side. I enjoy seeing where the levers of power are and how decisions are made.

**EISNER:** You are looking at it from the grandstand and taking notes; I was in there playing it. I love the scrimmage.

**MILLER:** You've been an employer many times in your career.

> "In talking to you, I do get a sense that there's the dreamer and then there's the *schemer*!"

**EISNER:** I've been an employer for most of my career. But I understand the marketing end of [publishing], and it gives me a chance to be with people. Because, as you say, sitting at that drawing board all day is a very lonely business. If you know nothing else and you have no other contact with other people, you become very warped in many ways. That's why a lot of cartoonists have trouble. If [Jerry] Siegel had had any sense at the time, all he'd had to do was get himself a lawyer [before selling the *Superman* strip]. He might not have gotten an ownership deal, but —

**MILLER:** He'd never have gotten ownership.

**EISNER:** Donenfeld would have had him killed before giving him that! Donenfeld was a little mafioso anyway. But a lawyer could have gotten Siegel a deal like Bob Kane got, which was some kind of a guarantee. All Siegel got was a promise: "Don't worry, we'll take care of you."

**MILLER:** I know *that* one. At least by the time I showed up, when they said that, everybody knew they were lying *[laughs]*!

> "Sitting at that drawing board all day is a very lonely business. If you know nothing else and you have no other contact with other people, you become very warped in many ways."

**EISNER:** When you showed up, it was a totally different time.

**MILLER:** They had to make us all take blood oaths by then, because your generation had turned around and said *hey!* a few too many times. Back in the seventies, we had to turn over our firstborn before we even got in the door!

**EISNER:** A lot of the artists were really helpless guys. They were so inbred, so wound up in their own little world. Wally Wood came into my office one day and said, "Will, you're the only guy I can turn to. You're something of a businessman. I'm getting screwed by Jim Warren." I said, "How are you getting screwed?" He said, "Well, he said he was going to publish this magazine of mine, and then he changed his mind, and now he's not going to publish it. Can I sue him? I'm going to sue the bastard. I'm going to kill him!" I said, "You can't sue Jim Warren. He's got a right not to publish your magazine, and you've got a right not to do it. Take it back from him and try to find someone else to do it. And Wally said, "So, *you* publish it." I told him I wasn't a publishing business anymore. I offered him some work. I'd started up this other company, it was eating up all my time, and I could no longer continue doing *The Spirit* the way I was doing it. I was working on *The Spirit* at night, I'd just gotten married, and Ann was screaming blue murder, so I asked him if he'd consider drawing *The Spirit*.

**MILLER:** Those were the outer space stories.

**EISNER:** Those were the outer space stories — and then he quit right in the middle of it! He said, "It's not for me; I don't want to do it." [Jules] Feiffer was writing the stories, and I was going over the thing.

**MILLER:** It's a fascinating collaboration.

**EISNER:** It was great. Wally was a genius. In 1950, he did space-ship interiors that were valid in 1980! I mean, thirty years ahead of his time!

**The outer space *Spirit*, in Wally Wood's unmistakable style. From "Mission ... the Moon."** *© 1952 Will Eisner*

**MILLER:**  I really, really adore Wood's work.  I think if I tried to distill what I love most about it … more than any other comic book artist I can think of, he was able to find the glamour in every subject.  Whether it was a woman's ankle or a piece of dog crap, he made it look *beautiful*!

**EISNER:**  The saddest thing about Wally Wood, in my opinion, is that he should have continued doing Wood nymphs.  He should have done what the Pinis are doing today [*Elfquest*].  He was wonderful when he did the little forest stuff.  Then he killed himself.

**MILLER:**  His fantasy work was pretty sexy stuff, too.

**EISNER:**  It had an erotic quality to it, but it was still very, very Woodsy and *good* fantasy.  Very beautiful stuff.  He was an example of what I'm talking about.  The artists really did kill themselves.  They had no way of dealing with the market as it was.  Neal Adams dealt with the market as it was, because he said, "I'm going to set up my own company and sell art to another place across the street if you don't give me what I want." Wood did not understand that, and he felt trapped by it.

> **"Wally Wood was able to find the glamour in every subject. Whether it was a woman's ankle or a piece of dog crap, he made it look *beautiful*!"**

Harlan Ellison wrote an article once for *Playboy* wherein he said that Wally Wood was destroyed by the industry.  Well, he wasn't destroyed by the industry.  Wally Wood destroyed himself.  He was destroyed by battering his head against his inability to deal with reality.

Most of the artists at that time needed a practical outlook, and many of them didn't have it. Joe Simon had a good, practical outlook, but Kirby didn't. Jack was a worker, and he thought of himself as a worker. He believed later that Stan [Lee] didn't deserve all the credit Stan was getting — at least he felt that — and he wanted some of it. But in a way he deserved more than he really got in his time. Nonetheless, he came to that conclusion too late.

## "Power is not given; power is taken."

**MILLER:** At the same time, I think it's a bit facile for us to say that everything would've been great if they'd known how to play the game. Well, most people don't. And a better system would have made happier people. I'm not saying the industry killed Wallace Wood or anything, but certainly a more equitable arrangement would've been healthier all around.

**EISNER:** Exactly, but a healthier arrangement does not come like the gentle rain from heaven. You have to get it. Power is not given; power is taken. Yes, they started to form unions, and unions didn't work because the artists wouldn't live with unions. Neal Adams's idea of a union didn't work. The National Cartoonists Society never wanted to create a model contract. The early syndicate contracts were *really* enslavement, if you want to talk about slave contracts. They owned the copyright. The contract gave the syndicate a right to give the work to someone else if they felt that you were incapable of continuing. If they caught you drunk one night, they said, "You're no longer able to continue this. We'll give this to someone else."

**MILLER:** Half the cartooning business would have been shut down over a weekend *[laughs]*!

**Former *Stars and Stripes* cartoonists assembled at the National Cartoonists Society meeting, September 1965. From left: Mort Walker, Dave Breger, Vic Herman, Will Eisner, Irwin Hasen, and Milton Caniff.** *Photo courtesy of Denis Kitchen.*

..................................................................................

**EISNER:**   That was the argument they used to give for why they had to own the copyright: because the newspapers were filled with guys who drank a lot, and the [editors] around the country would say, "I can't count on him giving me the strip every week unless somebody responsible owns it." So the syndicates decided they had the right to replace a cartoonist if he did something they or their client papers objected to. Those contracts were tough. Milton Caniff left Patterson[1] because Caniff wanted a piece of the ownership and the syndicate wouldn't give it to him. It was a constant struggle for cartoonists. At *Mad,* Harvey Kurtzman wanted equity but never got it.

..................................................................................

[1] Captain Joseph Medill Patterson, then head of the Chicago Tribune-New York Daily News Syndicate, which owned Caniff's *Terry and the Pirates.*

**MILLER:** It's an ongoing struggle, and there's an ebb and flow to it, too. At the time I came into the field, there were no rights to be had at the bigger publishers, and smaller publishers really were not taken seriously. No one thought they'd be around very long. Then came what felt like the revolution in the mid-eighties, when we got royalties and fans started seeking our names and all of us started getting a livable income.

Time passed and Hollywood got interested, and now it's become imperative to the publishers to control ancillary rights, because so much of the money available has to do with options and merchandising. Even the most liberal publishers are being more "boilerplate" about that stuff.[2] You have to have a lot of clout like I do to get the kind of contract that I've got.

**EISNER:** The point that you're making is a very good one, because it illustrates what's happening. The publishers themselves have to have enough power to be able to keep rights. If a guy comes along and the publisher gives him his contract and he says, "I don't want to work under this contract," he has somewhere [else] to go.

**MILLER:** On the other hand, the recent market has been sagging enough so that there's an awful lot of out-of-work talent. A lot of my friends are out-of-work comic book artists.

**EISNER:** *That,* my friend, is capitalism. That's what capitalism's all about.

**MILLER:** That makes it a buyer's market, and it changes all the rules.

**EISNER:** It's a buyer's market, and it *does* alter the rules, because the buyer is going to take whatever he can get. And right now that's very important.

---

[2] In regard to standard contractual clauses, that is.

# 22.....

# THE MEASURE OF SUCCESS

**MILLER:** When you came back [to comics], you always worked with smaller publishers.

**EISNER:** One of the reasons I always hung around with small publishers is because I could pick up the phone and call the guy who's making a decision. At big [publishing] houses, I pick up the phone and talk to a very sweet girl who doesn't buy the work.

**MILLER:** It's part of their corporate structure that you're never in direct contact with the person who makes decisions, so you're talking to someone who's frightened of the person above them, and they don't let you talk to that person. It's much easier for me if I know that I can go out and have a beer with [Dark Horse publisher] Mike Richardson.

..........................................................................

**Opposite: Will Eisner in 1981, with his former publisher and now literary agent Denis Kitchen. The rental car in the background is a Dodge Spirit!**
*Photo courtesy of Denis Kitchen.*

**Miller caricatured his *Sin City* publisher, Mike Richardson, in the lower right corner of this scene from *Family Values*.** © 1997 Frank Miller, Inc.

**EISNER:** Yeah, that's right. And, of course, there's another thing. You've become an important name to publishers because of your sales. I am important, but I don't make money for them; I give them prestige. That's what they're buying from me, and I'm aware of that. The books they sell of mine wouldn't even be a small percentage of what they sell of your books. So you're very important to them. I must compliment you — your books sell more copies than mine *[laughs]*.

**MILLER:** That's not the first time you've used that measure, Will. Earlier this weekend you were talking about a book, and you said you'd made ten dollars per hour on it — which surprised me, using that as the measure of success.

**EISNER:** No, it's not. I cited it to describe the investment. Sales are not my measure of success, but they're a publisher's measure of success. I'm confronted with it all the time. People constantly ask me how many copies of a book I've sold to the public; that's how much the book is "worth." My creative input is not sales driven.

But if you sell fewer copies than *X-Men,* then you're not as important to marketers as *X-Men.* This is what I'm talking about. As far as I'm concerned, my measure of success is the reader who responds, for example, "I don't agree with your concept of God. I'm a minister, and I want to tell you what I think." Or someone who writes to me and says, "Gee, I have an aunt just like that." Or the guy who said to me, "I just came back from America, and New York looks just like your books." That's my measure of success. But the practical measure of my success is that *A Contract with God* is still in print after 21 years. That keeps me going.

**MILLER:** I've had a couple of books that have had anniversaries, and the thing is, with the tenth anniversary, it really feels cool, because it's like, "Okay, the kid made it to ten. He's gonna be all right." The thing's still working for me.

I think whether or not the smart [readers] like it means a lot to me, too. That's my measure of success. When people describe a book as a vivid experience to them, or when I get a strong reaction — one that doesn't involve sharp objects!

**EISNER:** Who are the smart ones?

> **"Sales are not my measure of success, but they're a publisher's measure of success."**

**MILLER:** My peers. Also, among readers there's a certain type of reader who's a bit less likely to read superheroes but to still have a real love for adventure, for genre, who is also really interested in the form. And someone whose world is a little wider than the comic book world generally is. Someone who's aware of what's going on, because I play a lot to knowledge of contemporary events. I'm sure there are a great number of readers who, when *DK2* came out, had no idea who those people were, sitting around talking at the beginning, because I caricatured all those Sunday morning talking heads. And you have to be somewhat in touch with the culture to know who those people are. George Will is a mystery to them.

**EISNER:** How important are those caricatures to the essence of the story?

**MILLER:** Critical.

**EISNER:** If you don't know who they are, you can't understand it?

**MILLER:** No, you know that they're talking heads.

Television's "Sunday morning talking heads," featuring Miller's cartoon of George Will, from volume 2 of *Batman: The Dark Knight Strikes Again*.
© 2002 DC Comics, Inc.

**EISNER:** So, you don't need to know that this is a caricature of George Will?

**MILLER:** No, you don't have to know who they are, but it helps if you do, in terms of your enjoyment.

**EISNER:** What are the other indications of success? Money?

**MILLER:** Sure. Absolutely. But there's a ratio. The money becomes less important if I own [the rights]. When I did *Sin City*, I had no idea how it'd be received. The same with *300*. It didn't take nearly as many sales to make that one feel like a success as it does with something with the expectations of *Dark Knight 2*, which really had to be me putting on the uniform and hitting it out of the park in order to be anything but failure.

> **"You really are looking more toward the fine art or literary sensibility. What I'm up to is wanting to be part of pop culture."**

**EISNER:** Let me ask you, if the last book you did only sold nine thousand copies, would you consider that a failure? If *Sin City* only sold nine thousand copies, would you consider that a failure?

**MILLER:** Well, that would mean that a vast majority of my audience had gone packing — so, yeah, I wouldn't consider it very successful. That's an ongoing franchise, and you know you're gonna get a certain number of people in the house every time. I do see it as participatory, not just in terms of the intimate relationship between the reader and the comic, but I see myself as putting on a show.

**EISNER:** What you're talking about is performance. That's a marked difference between what I said a little while ago about my measurement of success and your measurement of success. My books don't sell two hundred thousand copies. They don't sell anywhere near that.

**MILLER:** Most of mine don't, either.

**EISNER:** Whatever the quantity is — eighty thousand, whatever. Those are large numbers, as far as I'm concerned. I'm just pointing out that's a major difference in our measurement of our own success.

**MILLER:** But I'm playing more to the kind of people who generally head to the comics shops. I'm doing stuff with broads, bullets; I think it's a rather intense variation, a move away from the traditional forms in comics, but it's in the same arena.

**EISNER:** I'm talking to a different audience, and it happens that the only arena I've had so far is the comic book shop. But I'm writing to a different audience; I'm hoping that somebody's mother will wander into the store. Or a couple of retailers I know who like my stuff frequently give a copy of one of my books to a kid and say, "Take this home to your mother and father, and if they don't like the book I'll give you your money back." I've been able to sell by word of mouth. So, my measurement is different; it concerns accomplishment. The work I've just done has to come out of my own need to say something and the comments I've gotten from somebody who may have read it and valued what I had to say.

**MILLER:** This gets back to our conversation about comics' role in the culture. Each of our takes is so different. You really are looking more toward the fine art or literary sensibility. What I'm up to is wanting to be part of pop culture.

**EISNER:** It's necessary in a conversation like this to define where we are going, because we're sitting here talking to each other across a fence

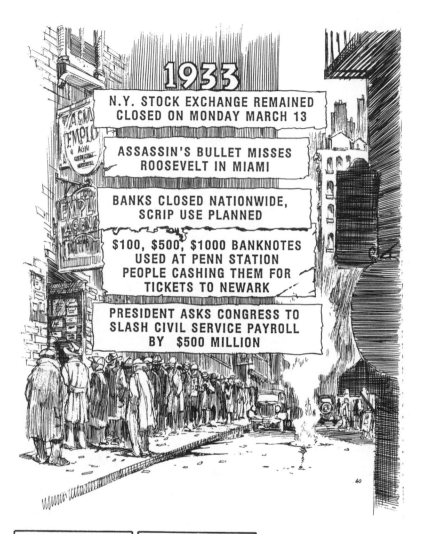

**Above: Eisner claims his work is "steeped in the past." From *A Life Force*.
© 1988 Will Eisner**

**Left: Miller's "perverse" portrait of the Reagan era, from *Batman: The Dark Knight Returns #3*.
© 1986 DC Comics, Inc.**

— or whatever the case may be.  The fence, in this case, may very well be the marketing.  I think a young reader reading our dialogue has to understand where we're coming from and what we regard as valid, because the young reader's measurement is based on what his peers say.  We were talking about this earlier.  One of the things we wring our hands over is the fact that society's measurement of anything worthwhile is how much money it makes or how much money it costs.

**MILLER:**  And the tide keeps rising.  The advent of the hundred-million-dollar movie raised the stakes in all of entertainment.  It had to be big, and big, and big — and incredibly powerful.

**EISNER:**  There was a time when there was a 64-dollar question, then it became a 64-*thousand*-dollar question.  Now it's *Who Wants to Be a Millionaire?*  So the values change.

**MILLER:**  And that surpasses inflation *[laughter]*!

**EISNER:**  I think that's a very important thing.  We are dealing with that.  I'm talking about a thing in society that's very subtle — and very traditional, maybe.  When you're addressing the family, you're addressing it on a totally different level than when I address the family.

**MILLER:**  Also, when I did [the first] *Dark Knight,* for instance, much of the satire in that book was my own perverse portrait of the Reagan era.  The new one is my portrait of the current era.  I like to interact with the current culture a great deal.  I enjoy the tension there.

**EISNER:**  And my work is steeped in the past.  It is, and I'd frankly rather write about the past, because it's there.  It won't change.  What's happening now is questionable.  It may alter right under my hand.

# 23.......

# NEW YORK

**EISNER:** In *The Big City*, what I wanted to do was make a portrait of all cities. In France they called the book *New York,* and ever since then the title has become *New York.* But, actually, I was talking about a portrait of any big city, because there are things in every city in the world that are pretty much the same. The fact is that people gathered in a city like that act and react [similarly].

**MILLER:** Yeah, and that's why I keep Sin City mythical. It changes climate. It really is whatever I want it to be. I let it change, like a human character. Cities are living organisms. For instance, there's a debate currently about what to do with downtown Manhattan, and there are several voices pleading to bring back the old grid that died when the Towers crowded it out. Because history has shown, since those towers

..................................................................................................
**Opposite: A plate from *City: A Narrative Portfolio.* © 1980 Will Eisner**

went up, that a city is on its streets, it's on its corners, and it's not in massive towers. It's on the human scale.

**EISNER:** That was my book! The city was the sewers, the curbs, the lampposts. Those are things we see. That was my argument. First of all, the city is a place that has become an area of danger. In the beginning, the jungle — the forest, where there are animals — was the area of danger. But we ultimately conquered the jungle. As civilized people we retreated to cities for safety. Originally that was the function of a city. We finally defeated the animals; as the Bible told us, we became sovereign over the beasts in the field, and we've replaced jungle with city. The city has become the jungle, the place of danger. And this is probably why your books resonate with the readers, because they've an instinctive feeling that the city is a place of danger.

> "A city is on its streets, it's on its corners, and it's not in massive towers. It's on the human scale."

But in my books, we're walking around the city amid lampposts, fire hydrants, and sewers. We see street corners, we see the bottoms of buildings. We don't see the tops of buildings, we never look up. The way to tell the difference between a New Yorker and a visitor is the visitor looks up and the New Yorker looks down on the sidewalk when he's walking. Those are two different views of the city.

**MILLER:** The beauty of a walking city like New York is that people have polite contact. It's hard to regard anybody as inhuman when you're living amongst every kind of person there is.

New York has always been a very romantic place in my mind. It was like the Emerald City to me, and it was also where they made comic books.

**Winter in New York, from Miller and Varley's *Elektra Lives Again*. © 1990, 2002 Marvel Characters, Inc.**

It was where you had to move, to get to make comics. I fantasized about the city. I read crime novels. My fascination started early and has been lifelong. Then I got to New York, and I really fell in love with it because I met such amazing people everywhere I went — the nicest people I've ever met, as well. It's a very kind place, and it's a fascinating place. And I can't get over the idea that this big sprawling place really is millions of stories happening at once. It's in people's eyes and the way they dress.

**EISNER:** Every one of those windows has a drama going on inside.

**MILLER:** Also, it's an intensely creative place. There isn't much about it that I dislike.

**EISNER:** Well, we both come from a different place. I come from the inner city. I don't see New York City the way you saw it coming in: seeing the skyline and listening to the music. I came from neighborhoods. To me, the city is a collection of neighborhoods.

Inside the subway train, from *City People Notebook*.  © *1989 Will Eisner*

Outside the subway train, from *Sin City: Sex & Violence*.  © *1997 Frank Miller, Inc.*

**MILLER:** Oh, yeah. Absolutely.

**EISNER:** And each of those neighborhoods is a world unto itself. In the neighborhood that I lived in, the world did not exist beyond our neighborhood. You didn't go to "Manhattan," you went to "New York" if you lived in the Bronx. This is a big difference. So, I see it differently.

**MILLER:** Living there, you do learn pretty quickly that you're in one village among a hundred thousand villages. There's no question about that.

**EISNER:** You're living in Manhattan. Greenwich Village is a neighborhood; Hell's Kitchen is a neighborhood. But you enjoy the ability to see the city as a whole. You're seeing it from the ferry boat; I don't see it from the ferry boat, and that's a big difference. Now you've lived there long enough that the total initial vision will change.

**MILLER:** It does change.

**EISNER:** Just like coming into a small town … I see this lovely little, sleepy little, wonderful little town, and after I've lived there for a while, it's no longer a sleepy little town. It's me and the neighbor next door. Big difference.

But back to the city. In my city, little things happen, not big things. My city is composed of a lot of little things. But the city has always been important in comics.

**MILLER:** Oh, yeah, all the superhero publishers were located in New York.

**EISNER:** I don't think that's why. I wouldn't attribute the development of the superhero to the publishers. I wouldn't give them credit for that. Superman was created by two guys from Cleveland, away from New York City. Their attitude towards New York City was like any other visitor.

But Gotham City … Bob Kane grew up where I did, so to him Gotham City was a major metropolis.

**MILLER:** But Metropolis and Gotham City were the light and dark versions of New York.

**EISNER:** Okay, but there was still a big city where these big things happen. Little things happen in my city. My guy sits on a fire hydrant and gets a ticket. Or … *The Building*, a book I did out of anger, because I saw a building being torn down. It was terrible to see this wonderful old building being torn down and this monstrous, glass-covered black box that was put up instead. I did the book when I was old enough to walk around the city and found myself missing an old building here and there.

The "building" in question, from Eisner's graphic novel of the same name. © *1987 Will Eisner*

**MILLER:** Here's a little sad life story on my part. I just moved back to Manhattan a little over a year ago [in 2001], and my new neighborhood is off 9th Avenue, which is a wonderful walking street. And one of the hardest things to find nearby in New York is a good pharmacy, because the Duane Reades have moved in and they're horrible places. They have plenty of merchandise, but you just don't want to enter them. It's surly hell. And right up a block from me was the Alps Pharmacy.

It had a beautiful art deco sign, and inside was this amazing couple, husband and wife, who had owned the place forever. You didn't really even need a doctor with these people. They were sweet as could be. One day I walked in and the wife had made sandwiches. I'd read that morning in the *Times* that they'd sold the place because a building was being put up. The couple was really sad about it. They would have been allowed to stay, but they just didn't think, at their age, they could live through a couple years of construction right on top of them. When that sign came down on that building and there was just a big hole there, it was heartbreaking.

## "Metropolis and Gotham City were the light and dark versions of New York."

**EISNER:** That's my book! But to return to the subject, the reason why the big city lends itself to the comics story, the comic book medium, is it is still a place of great adventure. Theater. A drama in every window. Millions of windows.

**MILLER:** Yeah. It's a place where tons of great moments happen, and also it looks great. It's hard to imagine what Superman would do in a cornfield in Kansas!

**EISNER:** Yeah. If Superman or Batman had his lair in a small city in Nebraska *[laughs]*, what kind of adventure would he have?

**MILLER:** Right. The city gives you everything. For one thing, the city, in particular, is vertical. Where else can you put a character who flies? How else would Batman get around? He'd be sitting in the Batmobile all day long!

**The vertical environment of the city influences the story set therein. From *The Spirit*.** © *1950 Will Eisner*

**EISNER:** Also, the environment affects your style. My stories respond to the environment. It influences my style, and yours. The stark black-and-white indicates city lighting. In the beginning, when I was doing *The Spirit*, I was obsessed with the vertical. Everything in *The Spirit* was either up or down. The guy who comes from a farm, his concept and vision are horizontal. Mine was in the vertical. So lighting was very important. Those were the graphic influences.

**MILLER:** One thing that I really feel got kind of lost for a long time there — which was present in some of the early comics artwork of New York City — for instance, *The Spirit* and the stuff Jerry Robinson created in *Batman*, much of the early stuff — the city was shapes. Massive shapes. As styles changed and comic book art got more photography-oriented, the detail started taking over and the scale was expressed by how many windows you could see, not with this monolith of a building with no windows. I really want to get back to boldly saying, "That's a big rectangle over there." That's what I love about the scale of it. I don't need to see all those little windows all the time.

**EISNER:** This is essentially what I was talking about earlier when I was talking about impressionism. You're dealing in impressionistic messages. I am still dealing with it. My buildings don't have detail; they only look like they've got detail. That's a big difference. Now there are people who do incredible detail. Did you ever see the work of Jacques Tardi, the French cartoonist? He's impressionistic, but you get a sense of enormous detail.

**MILLER:** If you look at Tardi and you look at Steve Ditko, they can tell you what city you're in by one little metal chimney!

**EISNER:** I didn't follow Ditko. But, anyway, there is an advantage in evoking an impression in the way you draw a set of buildings. Part of your storytelling skill depends on how much detail you put in. And it has to do with rate of story speed. Your [type of] story moves so fast that if you stop the reader and give him a wall with five hundred windows carefully done, you're going to derail the whole damn thing.

**MILLER:** I've made that mistake, and I've learned on the job that you have to take a coherent approach to the way you tell the story. I guess one of the things I get hung up on, in terms of pacing, is that for so many decades the comic books that most people would see were paced like a metronome. They never sped up, and they never slowed down. They were for so long the same number of panels and the same amount of words per panel. The "factory" stuff was like that. And, again, I think that there's a whole range of fun to be had once we get rid of that stupid pamphlet.

**EISNER:** I'm less interested in the amount of fun to be had; I'm interested in telling a story.

**MILLER:** They're not the same thing to you?

**EISNER:** No, not really. I don't do a story because it's fun to do. I've heard you say several times, "This would be fun to do" — but I can't afford that luxury right now. I enjoy doing a story the way somebody enjoys

Miller's city of sin is defined by shapes, not meticulous details. From *Sin City: The Hard Goodbye.* © *1991 Frank Miller, Inc.*

**Though fundamentally impressionistic, the work of French artist Jacques Tardi conveys the illusion of detail. From *Le Secret de la Salamandre*.**
*© 1981 Casterman*

telling a joke and everybody laughs. Or if I tell a story and people say it's great because they feel the effect of a story. But there is an enjoyment in the actual act of execution. *Minor Miracles* was a book I enjoyed doing more than any I'd done in a long time. It was the first time I had done this gray wash with the dirty water. And I was having such a good time doing it that, towards the end, it didn't really matter any more to me other than doing it well. I remember only the high of accomplishment. *Minor Miracles* was a series of short little stories that will probably have no endurance other than just being little stories. They have no great social significance, but the book was worth doing. But I didn't do it *because* it was fun to do. I did it because I wanted to tell what I thought *needed* to be told!

**MILLER:** I enjoy the performance. Beyond that, and this is probably going to sound like sacrilege, but I do have my imaginary audience in my head, and I am provoking them, and prodding them, and tricking them, going, "They're gonna hate this."

**EISNER:** That is the voice of a performer.

**MILLER:** What's the voice in your head when you're talking to your imaginary audience?

**EISNER:** I want to hear a sob. I want to tell them a story. I want to tell you about Carolyn Lamboli who killed herself a week before the welfare check finally arrived. I want to be able to hear you say, "Yeah. Jesus. Shit, man, I understand what you're saying." That's all I want from you. I just want you to know what I know. I don't want to shock you. I don't want to excite you. I don't even want to titillate you. While I do show sex scenes from time to time, I never do it in any way that is designed necessarily to be titillating.

**MILLER:** That's not a claim I could make *[laughter]*!

> "The reason why the big city lends itself to the comics story, the comic book medium, is it is still a place of great adventure. Theater. A drama in every window. Millions of windows."

**EISNER:** I don't know if that's a claim. Mine is not a claim; mine is a confession. It's an explanation. Mine is the act of a storyteller; yours is the act of a performer.

**MILLER:** I'm sorry, I think there's more than one kind of storytelling. I think it can be both.

**EISNER:** I don't deny that. I'm not saying this is an *evaluation* of what you're doing, but I'm telling you that we approach this thing differently. I'm a witness. I think of myself as a witness. There's a guy lying here

**Eisner's sexual scenes are few — and comparatively restrained. From *New York: The Big City*. © 1981, 1982, 1983, 1986 Will Eisner**

on a sidewalk, dead, and a bunch of people are just walking by, and I'm stopping one of them and saying, "Let me tell you about this guy. Have you noticed this fellow lying here? He just fell out of the window. Stop, let me tell you." I guess I'm the Ancient Mariner. I've just come off a ship where we have dead bodies all over the ship, and I want to tell somebody about that.

Inside me are a lot of stories that I feel a need to tell. These are things I've seen, and felt about, and I hope somebody else has seen them the way I have. And, yes, I'm as angry about it all as you are, in your own way, but my anger is part of the engine that's driving the telling of my story.

Every time I do a book, I realize I haven't quite done the thing as well as I really wanted to. I haven't got time to feel successful. Sure, I've got money now that I didn't have when I started. Sure, I can buy a Rolls Royce, but I don't need a Rolls Royce. I need to leave a footprint in the sand.

**MILLER:** You wouldn't last ten minutes in Hollywood, then.

**EISNER:** Hollywood is an environment wherein you're measured and judged by how much money you have. That's one of the problems with our society. People are too often judged by the amount of money they have. I'm not concerned with creating envy. I want to get my reader by his lapels, and I want to make him think and I want to make him cry because of what I'm telling him.

**MILLER:** What I want to do is make him stop breathing!

**EISNER:** The way I tell stories, I'm writing a letter to somebody. And I'm telling them about the past. I'm telling somebody what happened yesterday.

> "I want to get my reader by his lapels, and I want to make him think and I want to make him cry because of what I'm telling him."

**MILLER:** And I feel like I'm giving them a harassing phone call *[laughter]*!

**EISNER:** That's funny, but it's good. It's right on. That is a very understandable difference. I'm telling you what happened. I'm telling somebody right now, either somebody my age or somebody who's had enough life experience to understand what I'm talking about. Obviously in the medium I'm working in, I can't get into as fine a detail as Saul Bellow would get into when he's writing a description of a given scene. Comics have that limitation. An image has a great deal of limitation. There's a certain amount of depth that it cannot evoke without the experience of a viewer. My reader needs a certain depth of experience. Our narrative begins with a single image taken out of a seamless flow of images …

**MILLER:** And it's amazing what a picture *can* do. I had a real cartoon moment walking up 9th Avenue one day. Everybody was buzzing back and forth on a hot day, and there were a lot of people on the street. I was walking by a restaurant, and there was the most beautiful little rag doll just lying on the sidewalk. I leaned over and picked it up, looking to see if there was a baby carriage or whatever, and there was nothing in sight. And it could have been some little girl's favorite rag doll. It was beautiful. But I didn't want to steal it and take it home. So I sat it on the stoop in front of the restaurant, like I was taking care of it or something, and then walked off.

**EISNER:** What you just talked about is the kind of thing that I would spend two pages drawing.

**MILLER:** It was completely meaningless. Some little girl lost her doll.

**EISNER:** It was very meaningful. As a matter of fact, in *Graphic Storytelling* I extracted a well-known thing from Ernest Hemingway. He once said, "I can write a short story in six words." What are the six words? He said, "For sale: baby shoes, never used." What you just described is something that I would jump on. Now, whether you would stop your story … there's a moving vehicle that's racing down the highway. Would you stop that in time for this guy to get out of there? *[Miller laughs.]* No, you wouldn't. You've provided a wonderful visual example of the difference between us.

On the other hand, let's talk of the meaning of a visual image. That image of a man — picking up a baby doll, a rag doll, looking at it, looking around, seeing nobody, and putting it on the stoop — that has to be a classic set of images. The depth of that drawing comes from the reader's experience. The reason you and I are so entranced by that thing is because we have the experience needed to give it context. Now, somebody writing this in text will talk about the history of this thing or give you a whole page of narrative that describes the inner feelings of the man who picked the doll up. We haven't got time to describe his inner feelings. We must somehow imply them visually.

**From *Graphic Storytelling*, the companion text to Eisner's seminal *Comics and Sequential Art*. © 1995 Will Eisner**

..........................................................................................

**MILLER:** It felt an awful lot like a French movie.

**EISNER:** I think it's a classic act of humanity. This is not something that an animal would do. It's something that a human being would do.

But getting back to the issue of why I said that images have narrative limitations ... that story you told is a beautiful example of how imagery can evoke emotion. But we need the support of the reader to help define the *internal* motions that go into it. I could develop that onto two pages, shown by the kind of man standing there and how he picks up the doll. It could go several ways. It could be a man in a tuxedo with a top hat. Or it could be an old man in shabby old clothes. It could be an athletic-looking man. These are the images that would evoke story and the depth that we're talking about. That is called storytelling imagery. That's what I meant when I said images have limitations.

# 24.......

# BREAKING IN

**EISNER:** What motivates artists coming into this field? What's bringing people into this field? The thing you articulated earlier, which I think is very true, is the whole phenomenon of artists having the luxury to say, "I love this kind of thing," or "I want to do this thing even if it doesn't make me any money." When I started, all of my experience was used as a way of making a living. The average guy in the field always answered with a cliché: "I *can't* do anything else." The difference between them and you and me is that we don't *want* to do anything else. You're not doing this only because you have to make a living; you're doing this because you want to do it. Meanwhile, you are making a very good living at it.

**MILLER:** I very quickly determined that I didn't want to do anything else. I learned how to make a living at it. The time in the trenches of work-for-hire trained me in a set of skills that would do an awful lot of new people a lot of good now. Things like working methodically. Working the same hours every day. Focusing on exactly what you're up to and concentrating on the storytelling, rather than a particular obsession with visual flummery. Recognizing that you're constantly communicating through images and acknowledging that it's not movies and it's not "fine art." The beauty of a comic is that it's clear, direct communication. My work is getting simpler and more cartoony because I'm much more interested in communication now than in any illustrative value.

> "The time in the trenches of work-for-hire trained me in a set of skills that would do an awful lot of new people a lot of good now."

**EISNER:** We both share that; if you look at my work, that's exactly what's been happening, too. It's much more in love with the idea of being in service to the story. Gil Kane used to refer to *good* comic book art as artwork in service to the story.

**MILLER:** I have to say that when I started, nothing better could have happened to me than to be under a quota of producing a set number of pages and learning how to tell a story working with rhythm and making everything I could *count*. I could play with the actual pace of things. I became much better at my job. You have to become a professional.

**EISNER:** I agree. Under a severe deadline, if you are a professional at delivering, you learn how to do things efficiently. You also learn how to fake.

**MILLER:** Absolutely.

**EISNER:** And fakery in this business very often is very helpful. You learn that you don't have to put all 45 windows in that building; you just do one window. Feiffer once did a humorous sex sequence in *Playboy* that was all solid black panels with short balloons. Supreme, brilliant fakery.

**MILLER:** Also, one of the things that I tell people working on comics — especially newcomers, who find things so *precious* that the energy flows out of the project altogether — is that the reader is going to experience this much, much faster than you are. So keep that in mind. Comics move through time. They do not sit there like tablets.

**EISNER:** What's also very helpful is the solidity of the story. If it's a solid story that you're telling, then the manner of telling it is secondary to the actual telling of it. And I think that's a very important thing. A lot of times, the stuff you were talking to me about earlier — the rate of speed, the rhythm of movement — that's something you can do if there's an underlying, solid story. It's like good framework on a building: you can change the kind of architecture on a building anytime you want, as long as the solid structure is there.

> **"Fakery in this business
> very often is very helpful."**

**MILLER:** Even though the approach we take to telling our stories is very different and we have different procedures to getting there, we have set procedures. Because the last thing you want to do is do work that you won't use. You'd rather make a mistake in pencil than in ink. And the worst thing you can do is charge ahead of yourself, because then you start making mistakes, and mistakes will really kill you every time.

**EISNER:** Work ethic in this field is a very important question. When I talk of young cartoonists, the only exposure I've had to young cartoonists

**Like Miller, though clearly more influenced by Crumb than Kirby, Peter Bagge is of a generation of cartoonists who *wanted* to work in comics. From "Comics: A Young Man's Game?" © *2001 Peter Bagge***

was teaching at SVA [School of Visual Arts in New York]. None of them had a feeling of responsibility to the guy they were actually providing a comic for, the publisher. That's what I think the fan magazines capitalize on: the feeling that the publisher is the enemy.

**MILLER:** Or the *parent*, which is the much more corrupt notion.

**EISNER:** Well, actually, to the average cartoonist, the publishing house is a large womb and the father is the publisher. He's the guy we hate even though he pays our salary. But the idea seems to be: "What can I *get away* with?"

**MILLER:** Part of the fun of doing the old stuff is to push in the walls.

**EISNER:** That's just the creative part, and that's why I wondered what was happening when you said earlier that people working in the field now, or people like you, are in love with the medium and want to work in this medium. Because that's an exciting thing.

**MILLER:** We were nothing; we were just a handful. The energy coming in now and the numbers coming in now are just unprecedented.

**EISNER:** And they're in love with the medium itself. Is that really where it's going?

> "Now it's an actual career move to turn your name into a franchise."

**MILLER:** I'm just starting to catch up with what's happening. I've been off on my own for so long that things look to be a lot more interesting than I thought they were. I see two particular types of artists coming into the field. There are the ones coming in who really love the comics they grew up with, and their real dream is to draw *Spider-Man*. The best of those will eventually see their dreams through and then look up and go, "I've gotta do something with the rest of my life," and then come up with something of their own. But the rest won't. I think we're gonna have these old properties around for a long time, because they do have enduring appeal.

But the other group ... the more interesting artists are the ones who get into the art form. And they don't really care so much about *Superman* or anything as they do about getting ideas on paper and learning what a cartoonist does. The other thing that I'm seeing in comics right now is that someone will come along and do their time in the field, having fun with *Hulk* or whatever, as part of an overall plan to get an audience, and then

**James Kochalka's "utter joy" of cartooning. From "Very Nearly Real," published in *Top Shelf Asks the Big Questions*. © 2003 James Kochalka**

look to where to take that audience. They recognize that we're businessmen, and say, "I don't want a day job. *This* is what I want to do."

**EISNER:** That's a very interesting point, because something I have been struggling with is finding out what is in the minds of the people who came into the field after you. The guys who are coming in today, the kids at the Small Press Expo who are sitting there drawing their hearts out, a lot of them are imitative, a lot of them keep doing superheroes, but enough of them are not doing that so that I get a feeling something good is happening.

**MILLER:** Then there are the people who are doing the work-for-hire stuff sharply as a steppingstone.

**EISNER:** That's classic.

**MILLER:** Now it's an actual career move to turn your name into a franchise.

**EISNER:** That's a classic move. It's what I advise students to do. Go in, get a job, work on Batman or Superman or Spider-Man or whatever superhero the companies have got, until you're on your feet and make enough money to be able to go out and try your own. But ultimately you've got to take a gamble and have something to say. That's one of the things we should talk about, here: having something to say. What have these people got to say? The guys in San Francisco [the underground cartoonists] working around 1970 had something to say. What do these people have to say?

**MILLER:** I don't think there's a communal voice. Certainly there's a shared love of chaos. There's an adolescent fever pitch to some of the stuff, that I find quite dramatic. But as far as an overall message … some of them, like [James] Kochalka, are just in love with how the medium works and in making it work. Breaking it down. Sabotaging the "pretty, pretty" conventions of the current superhero stuff and getting back to the utter joy of a kid, his pen, and a stack of paper. We need the reminder.

ISSN 0712-7774

CEREBUS
GUIDE
TO
SELF
PUBLISHiNG

UT!

SIM 97

# 25.......

# PROFESSIONALISM

**MILLER:** What does that person walking into the field today have to do to break in? They're 23 years old, relatively good, and want to end up where we are. It's different than when I came in. What do they need to know about the business to successfully pull it off?

**EISNER:** There's a fundamental answer to that question. If they learn to think fundamentally, the answer will be right there. The business of comics or the business of art is a simple matter of marketing. You have something to sell; the publisher is looking to buy something he can sell. He represents the transmission of your stuff to an audience. The publisher's function is to look for an audience. The idea is to understand the various functions of different sorts of businesses. There's a publisher, there's a distributor, there's a retailer, and then there's the editor. Your

......................................................................

task is to sell to an editor, in the first place. There are only two things you have to sell: the idea and its execution.

Now, a lot of young guys coming in worry about getting screwed. It comes up a lot in the marketplace. But you don't get screwed unless you're standing there allowing it to happen. What happens is that if you come into a publishing house, you're coming up with two things. Either you must offer an idea, which the publisher may or may not accept, or you must offer your talent, the labor he is looking for. All the publishing houses are looking for a new Frank Miller, but they're thinking of the Frank Miller who *became* Frank Miller — the artist who walked in one day to [former Marvel editor-in-chief] Jim Shooter with a portfolio of his work, and Shooter thought, "This guy is good, I'm going to put him on a character we have here, and he's going to do it well." In the idea department, it's a little like winning the New York Lottery: the odds of selling an idea to a comic book publishing house today and retaining the ownership of it are quite hard. The only way to deal with that is to self-publish. For example, Batton Lash [creator of *Supernatural Law*] had an idea, and he decided to self-publish. He went through the agony of self-publishing. If you want to talk about the difficulties of self-publishing and the promise of self-publishing, talk to him or Jeff Smith [creator of *Bone*]. These guys really struggled, but they did it. Dave Sim [*Cerebus* creator] did it. It's possible to do, but you have to be willing to go that route. If you need to make quick money, if you've got a family and need a regular income, then go in and sell your drawing or writing ability instead.

Now, about getting screwed: it can happen if you're making a deal with somebody who violates his agreement with you. When you're submitting an idea, it can get stolen because a guy can look at an idea and say, "No, we're not interested," and then two weeks later out comes a strip just like yours. That's stealing, but very few publishers will do that today, because it's cheaper to buy the thing from you than to deal with a lawsuit later on. The way to avoid getting screwed is to understand that it's a give-and-take. It's a deal; get it in writing. You're giving them something, and they're giving you something.

There's another thing: *you* have a responsibility. You're a manufacturer. Each individual cartoonist is a manufacturer, a one-man factory, and if he promises to deliver five pages next week, he must deliver on that promise … he's responsible. Work-for-hire is very much like hiring someone to paint your house. "It's my house, I want you to paint it in the colors that I like, and when you finish, I own it." Very few architects own the structure they've designed.

> **"The business of comics or the business of art is a simple matter of marketing. You have something to sell; the publisher is looking to buy something he can sell."**

**MILLER:** I understand your point, but that sort of analogy always troubles me. The same way that it bothers me when people who are arguing for a labeling system of comics say, "It's a box of peas." There is a quintessential difference between something that's created and drawn in a comic book, and getting your house painted.

**EISNER:** I'm willing to listen. What did I say that you find objectionable?

**MILLER:** It's an analogy that ignores that there's a different *meaning* to the work than to painting a house. Yes, it is work that the other person will own the rights to, but it is still —

**EISNER:** I'll accept the fact that it's a highly simplistic metaphor. I'm talking now about the question of what the business approach is.

**MILLER:** I understand that.

**Miller's editorial comment on Marvel's resurrection of Elektra, the popular character created but not owned by the artist.** *Artwork © 1997 Frank Miller, Inc.*

**EISNER:** I used to run a sequential art class over two sessions, including a session about writing contracts. Making a deal. What should be in a deal? Every contract should have a beginning and an end, even if it's "in perpetuity." Also, it begins with something you're giving and what you're getting for what you're giving. Even with work-for-hire, if I'm going to do fourteen pages of your superhero, I'm giving you something, and you have to give me something back. This is not the world of "fine art"; it's commerce.

> "Make sure you know what ownership is. It certainly isn't just having the copyright."

**MILLER:** Absolutely. We're definitely in a situation where there are two ways of doing comics. First there was one, which was the straight work-for-hire deal. Then there were two, as the smaller publishers came along and rights became more negotiable, and all of a sudden royalties were paid. There was ownership and non-ownership. Now we've got kind of a menu of possibilities. What I want to throw in is to make sure … when you're coming in and you want to own your work, make sure you know what ownership is. It certainly isn't just having the copyright. Learn what a trademark is. Talk to a lawyer if you can. There was a time when ownership was getting easier, and now I foresee a time when it's going to go in very much the opposite direction. It's gonna tighten, because Hollywood's interested. You will technically own the work, but the publishers will have the ancillary rights forever. That's gonna be a standard deal.

**EISNER:** Let's stay on that — that's a very important point. What is ownership? You're right that ownership is not simply the ownership of copyright. Owning a copyright alone is meaningless. What a publisher is offering you, the creator, is marketing.  He says to you, "Look, you've got this wonderful idea, or you've got this marvelous talent, and I'm going to market this talent.  I will keep eighty percent, and I'm going to give you twenty percent.  You say, "No, I want thirty percent," and he says, "That's not a good deal.  I won't do it."  You're left with the property and the copyright, but you can't do anything more with it.  So, in that case, the copyright is meaningless.  There's no reason why a publisher would let you own a property.  He doesn't morally have to give it to you.  To Frank Miller he has to give the ownership, because Frank Miller won't do business with him any other way, and he needs you because you're making money for him.  It is not a moral issue.

**MILLER:**  It is really an uncomfortable thing to see what happens when people say, "I've got a copyright," and they might as well have just signed the work-for-hire agreement.

**EISNER:**  The copyright, as I say, is important, but it's meaningless in the marketing sense.  If you sell a property to a publisher on a work-for-hire basis … you create a new superhero and suddenly one day you discover the publisher is selling millions of copies while you're still getting only fifty dollars per page or whatever, you may regard that as being screwed, but you're *not* being screwed, because he didn't lie to you.  He said to you, "I'm going to give you fifty dollars a page for this, and I own it.  And I have the right to take a risk and market it."  There you have a *moral*, not legal, issue.

**MILLER:**  I don't brook much whining out of my generation, because we had your generation to show us what happened to all the people who went along with work-for-hire.  So we went in with our eyes open.  When I created a popular character under work-for-hire [conditions], I knew exactly what I was doing.  It's just that I do think it's important to know.

**EISNER:**  Also, let me add that from your point of view it may appear that the people of my generation were being screwed, but we weren't really being screwed because that was the marketplace. In those days when a guy worked for 75 cents an hour as a basic bottom line, we might think he was being exploited or being screwed, but that's from our present point of view. At that time, when I got five dollars a page, that was the standard market rate. I had a choice either to do it at five dollars a page or not to do it.

Bob Kane quit Eisner & Iger because I was paying him only five dollars a page, and Donenfeld offered him seven or ten dollars a page, so he went there. I wasn't about to give him ten dollars a page, because by then I was maybe getting about seven dollars a page, and I was making a dollar and a half markup for overhead and profit. It was the market then, just as the market is today.

**MILLER:** Right now, power is once again consolidating in the industry in the most frightening way it has in decades. When I came into comics, there were two big publishers. If there had been only one, I would have had no negotiating power whatsoever, but I was able to pull the prima donna, play one against the other, and enough of us were able to do that so that royalties did happen and publishers did compete for talent. That opened up a lot. Then came the wonderland of [multiple] publishers and self-publishing and other options, but that was also a time when there were a number of distributors. Now there's *one* comics distributor, and we're moving increasingly towards what could be a two-publisher industry — and that's not a healthy thing.

**EISNER:** Look at it from the other side, from the publishing side. If you want to be a publisher, you've got to deal with the fact that there's only one distributor. You've got to figure how to market your books with this one distributor, because there's nobody else to go to. If Steve Geppi [President of Diamond Comic Distributors, Inc.] offers to buy your books only at sixty percent off, period, then you've got no place else to go. There is nobody else. So, to answer your question about what the young cartoonist coming into this field has to face, the only way you can avoid being diddled or screwed is to understand the market. Take a look at the marketplace and understand what its realities are. I never subscribed to this Creators' Bill of Rights[1] because I believed that there was no reality to it. In the marketplace, moral rights are often disregarded.

> "Anybody who comes in thinking that artists should be miserable or poor is thinking like a *loser*, not like an artist."

**MILLER:** I think that was an attempt, much as Neal Adams has tried and much as you have tried, to change the [traditional] mode of thinking.

**EISNER:** Well, there is no ingrained right; there are no God-given rights here. The rights are what you negotiate.

**MILLER:** Well, that's just the thing. You can't say you don't have the right to sell your property.

**EISNER:** Well, in France you can't. You can't divest yourself of a property. You can only license it for 99 or a hundred years, but you can't divest yourself of the property itself. Just as there are "moral rights" to selling a painting: I can sell you a painting of mine, you can buy the painting, but you have no right to paint a mustache on that thing and alter it in some way. And I sell it with certain limitations. You can't make Spirit condoms, for example.

[1] The Creators' Bill of Rights was Scott McCloud's thirteen-point follow-up to a "Creative Manifesto" drafted in 1986 in Toronto, Canada, at a meeting hosted by *Cerebus* creator Dave Sim and attended by *Teenage Mutant Ninja Turtles* co-creators Kevin Eastman and Peter Laird, among several others.

*1.* "The right to *full ownership* of that which we *fully create.*"

*2.* "The right to *full control* over the creative execution of that which we *fully own.*"

*6.* "The right to employ *legal counsel* in any and all transactions."

*8.* "The right to *prompt payment* of a *fair* and *equitable share* of profits derived from *all* of our creative works."

**Four of the thirteen rights from the Creators' Bill of Rights drafted by Scott McCloud, illustrated in *Reinventing Comics*. © 2000 Scott McCloud**

**MILLER:** It's a mixed bag, but you have to address the business because it's related to all the other issues. The lovely moment that you're satisfying yourself at the drawing board, that's not done in a vacuum. It's part of how you create your life, and anybody who comes in thinking that artists should be miserable or poor is thinking like a *loser*, not like an artist.

**EISNER:** That's exactly right.

**MILLER:** And you can't think you'll blow it, because then you *will* blow it, and you'll be broke.

**EISNER:** I used to create a scenario for students in a business class. I always said to them: "Look, you create a character and you sell it to a publisher or to a syndicate. You've got the copyright and they're paying you royalties; it's not work-for-hire. The demand is getting heavy, you've gotta turn out six dailies and a Sunday strip each week, so you need help. So, you hire this guy, a young artist; now he's working for you, and he's emulating your style. You hired him on the basis that you own everything that he's working on. In a sense he begins to feel that he's being screwed, because he's contributing ideas, new characters, and stories … and it's all yours. What does he do?"

**MILLER:** What I like is that now these are discussions that are actually being had. They *weren't* being had when I came into comics. There was one law — it was like negotiating with Stalinist law — that was just the way it was done. I don't mean to vilify that whole time, because I had a great time.

**EISNER:** And you survived.

**MILLER:** I was decidedly the right age to enter the field at that time. I was nineteen, and when I came in it was the late seventies, and I got to see and be instrumental in changing a system that was falling apart. The sales were so low that people were convinced it was all over. It was an exciting time, because I got through my "boot camp" when I was exactly the age not to mind.

**EISNER:** A wonderful way to get into a business is to get in at the ground floor when it's in trouble.

**MILLER:** It was in deep decay.

**EISNER:** Good fortune is a great part of the reason for success. I was lucky to have arrived at the time I did. Had I arrived twenty years later, I might not have created the things I did. I might not have been as innovative as I was. I was innovative because there was nothing else around.

**MILLER:** Part of the quality of the *Spirit* stuff is that this is where your relative inexperience gives it a lot of its appeal. That's what a lot of these new comics are like. They're going, "Let's try this!" Like you did in *The Spirit.* "Let's move the type around here. Let's do something really crazy with the lettering." Those three-dimensional logos and all …

That's the, excuse me, but that's the spirit I've seen coming out of a lot of the young stuff. A lot of it doesn't work, but, God, are they trying! Artistically, their eyes are open.

**EISNER:** Are we saying that the new talent coming into the field has a better understanding of the business of comics than people did when you came in?

**MILLER:** I can't really address that, but I suspect not. The business doesn't know *itself* right now.

**EISNER:** See, the fan magazines have always perpetuated the idea that artists can be screwed. Can be cheated. And I never fully subscribed to that. I understood that they could be, but they could be only because they allowed themselves to be — because a guy said, "Take my word for it, I'm going to take care of you," and they said okay! Artists have the right — and must ask — that [the deal] be put in writing.

**MILLER:** Another thing is that people who come in often don't know the stakes. They either thought or they think, "Oh, well, there'll never be a movie of this anyway." And then if one gets made, they retroactively say, "I never agreed to that." There's a lot of that.

**EISNER:** I suspect that young people coming into the field now don't fully understand what it is they have to ask for. For example, I used to pose this to my students: "Look, you walk into a publishing house, you want to show your work to an editor, and the girl at the desk says, 'Mr. Brown is not in right now, but if you leave your portfolio, he'll look at it later today. You can come back tomorrow, and he'll make a judgment.' So what do you do?" And my student says, "Well, I'd leave my portfolio and then go." I said, "Do you ask for a receipt?" "Well, no, why should I ask for a receipt?" "Well, let me tell you what happens. The following day you come back, and the girl is not there. There's *another* girl sitting there, and you tell her you left your portfolio yesterday at two o'clock in the afternoon. And she tells you that *that* girl quit yesterday. She denies knowing anything about your portfolio." What I'm trying to point out is that there's a human relationship endemic in this field. Artists are afraid to offend the person who's buying from them, fearing that he might not buy their work because of it.

**Opposite and above: Classic examples of Eisner's innovative three-dimensional**
*Spirit* **logos.** *© 1949 Will Eisner and © 1948 Will Eisner*

*Photo by Charles Brownstein.*

**MILLER:** There are a lot of different, childish attitudes that come in, partly because the publishers do tend to be older and more —

**EISNER:** But remember, most of the guys coming in aren't dealing with publishers, they're dealing with editors. They're no longer sitting face-to-face with Harry Donenfeld.

**MILLER:** It's cyclical. It seems now, because sales are down, it's harder to get published, it's harder to get work off the ground unless you're really established. So editors are becoming more powerful again. They were very powerful when I first came into comics, because there was very little work to be had. They got steadily weaker as we inmates took over the asylum. But now they've steadily become as powerful as they were before. Now if you're a *Batman* editor or a *Superman* editor, you simply sit down at a convention and a line of people want to buy you a drink and beg you for work!

**EISNER:** That's an interesting point. How much can an editor of a *Batman* book or a *Spider-Man* book do? What can he do for me as a young cartoonist? Can he give me work?

**MILLER:** Yes. There might be a step or two, depending on the company, but editors do have a lot of leeway that way. And they know it. It's changed that way. I've worked with every kind of editorial situation imaginable, short of self-publishing. I came in when the editor was very powerful and had absolute say. The editor-in-chief [spoke] through the editor, as it was at Marvel. So I would negotiate with Jim Shooter.

**EISNER:** Were you concerned about offending Jim Shooter? Earlier you said that Jim Shooter told you what he wanted. So, if he told you to stop doing balloons your way and only use round balloons, were you afraid of saying, "I think that stinks; I only want to do square balloons"? Were you afraid of him saying, "Well, that's tough; you're going to do it my way — or goodbye"?

**MILLER:** I knew he had that prerogative, but I never let the conversation go that far. I would protest and argue, and we had some loud [conversations], but I didn't want to lose my job, certainly not over something like the shape of a word balloon.

**EISNER:** I realize that, Frank. What we're talking about is the relationship between the young cartoonist and the editor. A number of years ago my neighbor's grandson wanted to come by and show me some of his work. I said to my neighbor, "I don't buy anything, but I'll be glad to give him advice." He showed me his work, and it was pretty good. So I told him there was a convention nearby and that I'd introduce him to Dick Giordano [former DC Comics editor-in-chief]. I brought this kid along with me and told Dick to look at the work. I told Dick I thought it was pretty good, and Dick agreed with me. He thought the kid was ready [for publication]. So the kid was up at DC the following week, and they gave him pages to pencil. This was one way of getting into the field, but the kid was selling his skills and talents at the time, and editors were buying that way. Later, I heard that the kid was dropped because he sassed someone there.

**MILLER:** My first comic book gig was a variation on that, though I never got fired for shooting my mouth off. Never. But, like your neighbor's grandson, I had been bothering Neal Adams and bringing in my portfolio, and for a while he kept telling me how hopeless it was. And then one day I brought the stuff in, and he went, "Okay." And he called up an editor at Gold Key Comics. Access is the issue. Access is everything.

## "The climb from mailroom to writing comics is well-worn!"

**EISNER:** The formula I was always handing out was that if you're a writer, get a job on the staff of a publishing house.

**MILLER:** That has not changed a bit. The climb from mailroom to writing comics is well-worn!

**EISNER:** But now, the guys who tell me they're writers … I advise them to find an artist and then bring in samples. To artists, I tell them to find a writer. The team idea, I believe, is a very good way of getting in. The best comics are made when the writer and the artist are in one body. But short of that, from a practical point of view, the best way of getting started in the field is to create and publish your own stuff. The reality of today's marketplace is that the average publishing house is buying a huge amount of stuff. You're not going to be able to write and draw comics in enough volume.

**MILLER:** The problem is the format. It doesn't make any money, it doesn't work, it's bad for the form, and it makes it a strange, deadline-oriented periodical in what is no longer a magazine market. The standard comic book is gone. Publishers print too many titles because the comics make so little money that they have to print forty titles to make a buck each.

One thing that really helped, from my point of view, is the intimate nature of the industry. You can meet all the different forces in the industry. The thing that informs my basic view of professionalism is it has to be based on honesty and keeping promises. And watching your back, of course.

The biggest professional lesson I got was many years ago when I met a retailer who was angry about a book of mine that had missed shipping. And I came to realize that it wasn't just that I was displeasing the publisher by being late on something; it was that I was breaking a pact with the retailer, the distributor, and all these readers. And since then I've become a maniac about schedule.

> "The best comics are made when the writer and the artist are in one body."

What's going on right now with the lateness of things is disgraceful. I must say, however, that the publishers have been pretty damn negligent on that point, too. They seem to schedule by looking at the entrails of beasts!

**EISNER:** Is it that, or are they victims of the artist? I know of a case of a packager who was putting a book together, and he began with an artist who delayed him for so long that he lost his contract with the publishing house, because the artist kept delaying, getting money, and delaying. I felt that was an unconscionable lack of professionalism by the artist.

**MILLER:** There isn't anything that involves creativity without a certain number of unexpected developments occurring within a certain reasonable range. You say, "I'll have it for you in a month and two days." That's within the common range. But I try not to let those two days happen. That's different.

**EISNER:** That's time management. I say I do a page a day, but I don't know how long the next page will take me. I can't promise that. Another aspect of professionalism besides delivering on promises is the ability to deal with the vagaries of the marketplace. If an editor says to you, "This won't sell," you have to decide at that point whether you're willing to accept that and tailor the work to respond to the needs or taste of that publisher for whom you're working. Or whether you'll fight.

**MILLER:** That depends first and foremost on who owns the property. If you own the property, as the author I think it's perfectly professional for the author to say, "I'm not gonna do that."

**EISNER:** Is the definition of professionalism the ability of the author to factor in the realities of the medium, the marketplace, and the publisher's judgment? On the other hand, there is the question of what the editor's request will do to the author's image.

When you're working for a publisher, which is separate from working for yourself, the editor tells you, "We're going to need to change that sequence. We can't publish anything about homosexuality. Our publishing house doesn't deal with homosexuality." You say that your story depends on a homosexual relationship between these two people. He says they can't accept it. At this point, you've got to be able to deal with that problem as a professional. How important is that to you?

**MILLER:** That's a natural and healthy tension that exists. There should be a certain amount of tension, because publishers by their nature tend to be conservative and artists by nature tend to be leaping forward. The publisher's gonna have the final word. He's not gonna print stuff because you threatened him.

**EISNER:** What we're talking about is not who has the final word, but what professional conduct is under those conditions.

**MILLER:** If the disagreement is serious, you've got two ethical options. One is to negotiate until some agreement is made. The other ... if it's really serious, then it's moral to resign.

**EISNER:** Professional conduct, from the editor's point of view, is that it's professional of you to accede to the restrictions he's putting on this thing. If I'm the editor and you're a pro, I'm hiring you to do this, so it's professional of you to do what's requested. There is such a thing as professional conduct.

**MILLER:** Another thing that is a factor is that there is no God-given right to creative freedom, especially when you're working on somebody

*Photo by Charles Brownstein.*

else's character.  Once you have a track record that establishes you as somebody who can generate successes, your voice becomes much more powerful and you do tend not to have as many conflicts.

When you do get to the point that you have that kind of say, you always have to respect the client.  If you don't show a client respect, then you shouldn't be doing business with him.  I don't believe in sadomasochistic business relationships.

Doing business implies mutual respect.  If you have authority within the field, your position is different than if you're a first-timer.

**EISNER:**  If you've established your position in the field, by then you have probably all the professionalism necessary, otherwise you wouldn't have survived in the business at all.

**MILLER:**  I heard a completely reasonable remark from an editor of work-for-hire books who said, "Especially these days, when the market doesn't favor the talent as much as it did a few years ago, if you're doing work-made-for-hire, you've got to be *two* of three things: really terrific, on time, and easy to deal with."

**EISNER:**  Every professional is aware of that line where you withdraw. But at the same time, understanding what your client needs is part of the professionalism that's required — as well as the ability to accept a reasonable modification.

A lot of young artists harp about creative freedom.  They say their creativity is warped by editorial control.  "I want to free myself," says this young cartoonist, "of editorial control."

**MILLER:**  Part of that does have to do with age.  In a certain era in one's life, one is going to be rebelling against anything close to a parent figure or authority.  Sometimes that's just gonna happen.  But if it's work-for-hire, you're standing on water.  You've got no claim.

**EISNER:** There's something else again. One area that's never really touched on is the artist's responsibility to himself or herself. There are certain things that certain artists would not do. Artists have to know where that line is, because most of the time guys will say, "I don't give a damn; he's paying for this thing, and I'll do anything as long as I get the money out of this thing." So, there's a difference between creative freedom and the responsibility you have to yourself. A published author or writer has responsibility.

> "There is no God-given right to creative freedom, especially when you're working on somebody else's character."

To illustrate, here's another exercise I did with my students. Our class consisted of maybe three or four different ethnic groups. Blacks, Hispanics, Asians, whites, mixed religions, a mixed group. I asked them: "What if I were to walk into your studio and say that I wanted to buy a comic book from you and I was willing to pay a thousand dollars a page? I'd give you a script to work from, but beyond that, you could do what you wanted; you had complete creative freedom. Would you take the deal?" Most everyone said okay. But then I started reading the script, and it talks about "superior" people, that there's a group of people who are "superior" and a group of people who are "inferior." So then I asked the students if they could handle that, and now ninety percent said okay. Then I said that later in the script, you find that characters with dark skin are going to be eliminated and all the people with white skin are going to remain, because they are the "superior beings." Now the hands, especially African-Americans', started going down. So, finally, I said, "Okay, look, you don't need to sign your name to it, and I'll raise the

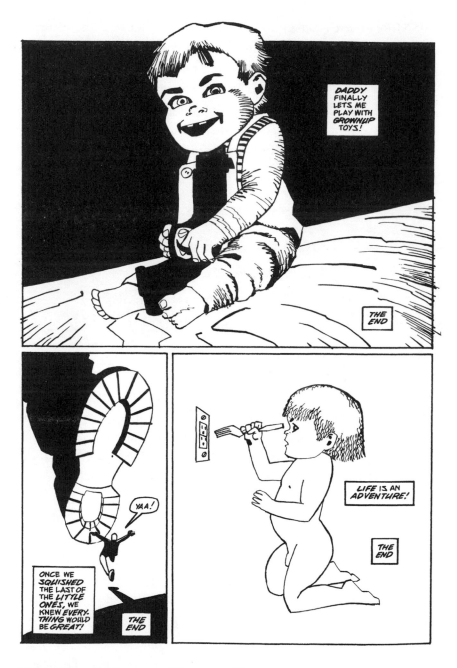

**Miller enjoys pushing people's buttons while at the same time pushing the medium's boundaries.  From "The End," published in *Dark Horse Maverick: Happy Endings*.  © 2002 Frank Miller, Inc.**

ante to *two* thousand dollars a page: 32 pages, you can do it in a month, that's $64,000 for a month's work! No one will ever know you did it; in fact, I'll sign *my* name to it." At that point the classroom erupted into a verbal free-for-all!

This is where we get into a sense of personal responsibility for what you're doing, and this is a very important part of what's going on in the field today. I wonder if anybody cares about what they're doing to the psyche of the public. They're interested only in how many copies a book will sell. The question becomes: What is the responsibility of the young cartoonist himself to the public? When will he say he *won't* do something?

**MILLER:** You have to make a decision. There are a number of things I won't do, but I wouldn't make that decision for anybody else.

**EISNER:** We're not talking about Frank Miller.

**MILLER:** No, but that was true of me when I was young. There were certain places I wouldn't have gone. But back then, they wouldn't allow much that could offend anybody. My problem was getting them to *let* me offend people!

# THE EDITOR
"I like it when you call me 'Ma'am.' I like it a lot."

frank MILLER

HELL
and BACK

A SIN CITY love story

TRADE PAPERBACK ON SALE NOW

DARK HORSE MAVERICK

# 26.....

# EDITORS

**EISNER:** How do you work with your editors?

**MILLER:** With the stuff that I own, there are endless course changes in plotting, so I just keep them informed. The editor is always kept abreast of where the project is at, and he or she is responding along the way.

Here are the two situations with an editor. An editor in a work-for-hire situation is working for the publisher and may be your advocate on certain points. But the chain of command is very clear. His employer cuts the checks.

In a situation like I have with Dark Horse, the editor's role is more ambiguous, because this person — Diana Schutz, in this case — is more like my partner, but also a liaison and a muse. She is involved in the process, and there's a mix of things she does — from cheerleader to proofreader to critic — that all get involved. Sometimes hardly at all and sometimes very much. I like having that relationship; it keeps the project alive. It keeps me on my toes. And it's good to be told when you're utterly off course. Nobody's infallible. I've never really understood this visceral dislike of any kind of dignified role for anybody but the artist.

**EISNER:** To me, the role of the editor is the surrogate of the reader. An editor's function is to be the reader and tell me when he doesn't understand a passage. On my last book my editor said, "I don't like anybody in this book." I look for that *reader's* point of view. By the way, how do you deal with deadlines?

> ## "It's good to be told when you're utterly off course. Nobody's infallible."

**MILLER:** I worked out something with Dark Horse that has turned out to be the perfect solution. *That Yellow Bastard* ran longer than it was planned, and I didn't produce it at a monthly clip. It started getting a little dicey a few months before the end of the project. So I said, "When do you need it?" and I started hearing a number of different options. So I called up [Bob] Schreck [Miller's then-editor at Dark Horse] and I said, "Here's an idea: Why don't you give me one date, the no-excuses date. It's the date when you calculate all the things that might go wrong and nobody on staff will have an excuse for delaying this if I meet that date." I asked Schreck to make it as late as he could, but with enough time so that Dark Horse had a comfortable amount of time to do what they needed to do.

**EISNER:** Did you know how many pages you had to do?

**MILLER:** I knew how many pages I had to do; I just didn't know how much time I'd have.

**Frank Miller and *DK2* editor Bob Schreck at SPX 2002. A typical moment between an artist and his editor!** *Photo by Diana Schutz.*

**EISNER:** Why did you put your head in the noose without knowing … ?

**MILLER:** Because I didn't want my book to ship late. I was on a roll, it was a double-sized last issue, and I beat the deadline by two days. But the deadline made for a much more vigorous issue, and my book shipped on time.

**EISNER:** I think what we need to do here is define how we measure a date. I'm enjoying the luxury of not having to make a commitment, other than saying I'll do a book this year.

**MILLER:** That's my situation now.

**EISNER:** *The Name of the Game* was [originally] estimated to be done sometime during the summer. What you saw me doing there [on *Fagin the Jew*] … I've done ninety pages, and I have 64 pages yet to go. So far, the page you saw took me a day to do — that's pencilling, inking and wash, and lettering the board. Now, depending on the rest of the book and the complexity of all those pages, I should be able to complete it in another seventy or eighty working days. "Working" days meaning five days a week. So I calculate on that basis. I still think the way I did when I was doing *The Spirit*, when I had six days to do a story. I know now, on this book [*Fagin*], given good health for another ninety days, it'll be three months before I'm able to deliver. I will not promise it to a publisher otherwise.

Now, *The Name of the Game* came out later than I'd originally thought.

> ## "To me the role of the editor is the surrogate of the reader."

**MILLER:** What I normally do now is just tell the publisher what I want to do, and then I go off and do it. Then I work with the editor all the way through it.

**EISNER:** At what point do you promise the editor the delivery?

**MILLER:** Now that I'm not serializing the stuff — only when I'm certain.

**EISNER:** At what point do you feel certain?

**MILLER:** When I'm well into the inking. What was so heartbreaking about having *DK2* come out late is that when you're dealing with a periodical schedule, there are many things that happen …

**EISNER:** What interfered with the production of that book?

**MILLER:** There was a lot of consternation over some of the material; that became quite an issue and delayed the book for a few weeks.

**EISNER:** Between you and the editor — or you, yourself, deciding what you wanted to do?

**In addition to the horrific events of 9/11, concerns over some of the material in**
*DK2* **and the huge publicity focused on Miller's return to the Dark Knight all**
**combined to delay the last volume of the series.  From volume 2.**
*© 2002 DC Comics, Inc.*

**MILLER:** No, between me and the *publisher*. That delayed some of it.

**EISNER:** Did you have to redo any of it?

**MILLER:** No. There had been concerns about the schedule, and just when it seemed like we knew the situation and everything was going to be fine, those airplanes flew into those buildings and things got very strange in New York. See, what I wanted to do was have the series done before the first volume came out, precisely because I knew that what I was doing would get a generally strong reaction, and there was a lot of publicity to do along the way. And I know how hard it is to work under those conditions, and then because I wasn't quite done, it became an out-of-control situation. I hadn't had a book come out late in, like, eleven or twelve years.

**EISNER:** I find this conversation very interesting because a good portion of my life was spent in a packaging operation where I had a bunch of people working on staff. We'd sell a book, and I'd have to calculate how much time it would take my staff to get it done by a certain date. The people producing magazines have to have a way of calculating the time they spend.

**MILLER:** I do want to clarify some of this, so it doesn't sound like excuses. There were delays on my end [with *DK2*], especially once the publicity started and reactions came.

**EISNER:** What were those delays?

**MILLER:** Mostly I was listening to the reactions, and that threw me off my game a bit.

**EISNER:** I'm a little confused about that. People called you while you were working in the studio and told you they wanted to interview you?

**MILLER:** No, they called DC Comics.

Miller's cover to *The Comics Journal* #209, lampooning the critics.
© *1998 Frank Miller, Inc.*

.........................................................................................

**EISNER:** And DC said, "Would you give so-and-so an interview?"

**MILLER:** Yeah.

**EISNER:** And so you'd take time out from the work you were doing.

**MILLER:** Often to go meet somebody for an interview.

**EISNER:** So you'd put in a half-hour, an hour on the boards, and the rest of the day was shot.

**MILLER:** Yeah. The other thing I wasn't used to, because I haven't been working as long-form as I want to, except for *Family Values*... I really had not estimated the sheer scale of 240 pages done that way. It was a job I learned a lot on. But it's really unfortunate that it didn't make the schedule.

THE FIRST THING I DID WAS KICK BEN AFFLECK'S ASS.

YEAH, I TAUGHT THAT PRETTY BOY A FIGHT MOVE OR TWO.

THEN JENNIFER GARNER FELL INTO MY HANDS LIKE RIPENED FRUIT.

NOTHING ON THIS PAGE IS TRUE.

# 27.....

# HOLLYWOOD

**MILLER:** You touched on something I have to agree with. Somewhere down the road, the notion of pandering became a virtue. It's *sanctified* in Hollywood! They actually show their stuff to focus groups of people with little meters on them to see whether they like it or not. And if their attention wavers, they cut something out of the movie. If later they say the dialogue at the ending is wrong, they reshoot the ending. So ultimately they've got something that pleases the broadest number of people.

**EISNER:** But that's determining market acceptability rather than the ethical value of the work.

**MILLER:** And it leads to creating something of no worth.

**EISNER:** Let's talk about Hollywood. Hollywood is Mecca now. As a matter of fact, that's why a whole bunch of guys led by Jack Kirby and Gil Kane all moved out to Hollywood at one point. When we moved down here to Florida, they moved out there.

**MILLER:** Jack went out there to work in animation.

**EISNER:** Well, that's Hollywood.

"Somewhere down the road, the notion of pandering became a virtue."

**MILLER:** Yeah, but they came on as hired hands. It seems to me that most of them didn't pursue real feature animation.

**EISNER:** No, that wasn't the main thing.

**MILLER:** If we're gonna talk about Hollywood, I think what it gets down to here is what's smart. I think the comics business is generally really, really stupid about Hollywood. If you're gonna sell your tail on the street corner, at least get some good money for it.

**EISNER:** Are you saying it's a question of how much money they're getting?

**MILLER:** I'm not going to decide whether it's the right thing to do. I'm just saying what's smart. Hollywood brings a lot of money to the table. That is the one thing we know will survive. You really have no way, unless you're making the movie yourself, to have a guarantee about the quality of what they put out — and it's very hard to get any kind of creative control. So if comics is a Research and Development branch, as was said to me by one of my publishers, we should at least be getting paid like one.

See, in Hollywood the stakes are very, very high, and there are a great number of people involved. The studios are spending a hundred million dollars on something, and that raises the tension. So they have a harder time generating and seeing through a really fresh and individual idea. It's just human nature when the stakes are that high.

So when they see all this stuff popping out of comics with all of this outrageous variety, they want it. But they see us as this starstruck little business that'll do anything. They're getting us cheap.

**EISNER:** That assumes that "us" is in control. You're right, Hollywood sees us as a source of creativity. Comics artists do what comes first, before a movie is made. Movies *adapt*; they're not creative. They take a novel and adapt it to film. They take a comic book and adapt it to film.

> "I think the comics business is generally really, really stupid about Hollywood. If you're gonna sell your tail on the street corner, at least get some good money for it."

**MILLER:** But here is where I think we're not taking advantage of it. As a culture, comics *is* starstruck when Hollywood wants to make a movie.

**EISNER:** Are you saying the cartoonist acts that way or the publisher does? There are two levels here: Jeff Smith who owns a property and negotiates, then there's DC or Marvel negotiating a deal. I don't think the major publishing houses are walking around with a little tin cup waiting for a movie house to come to them; I think they make fairly good deals. Are you saying the comic book houses are walking around with that feeling of self-loathing?

**Both Miller and Eisner caution against thinking of the movie industry as a step "up" from comics. From *Sin City: Hell and Back* #9. © 2000 Frank Miller, Inc.**

**MILLER:**  Yes.  Will, I've worked in Hollywood from time to time.  I lived there for a while; it's an amazingly glamorous place.  The weather is beautiful, the women are gorgeous, the cars are great, and the movie business is the glitziest thing in entertainment.  And, yeah, comics does tend to come in with its hand out — and it has, historically.  And to address your question of how publishers interact with Hollywood: publishers often decide whether or not to do a comic book depending on (a) whether they get a movie deal and (b) if they can control the rights. The silver screen is the badge of self-respect they've been crying for.

**EISNER:**   Do you think it's the big money that people are going for? Or does it mean that if I got a movie made of my comic strip, I've "arrived"?

**MILLER:**  The latter.  And in many, many, *many* cases, that comes with the hope that I can finally get out of this "ghetto" and work in "real" entertainment.  That's not how *I* feel, but I think there's a lot of that.

This brings it back to the work-for-hire issue.  When I work for Hollywood, I have a jolly good time.  It pays real well, but I know I'm a hired gun.  And exactly the same ethics of professionalism apply to that as to work-for-hire comics.  It's a different relationship than when I'm doing *Sin City*.

**EISNER:** Being professional is understanding and working within the area that's cut out for you.

**MILLER:** Yeah. But, in Hollywood, I've found the situation to be agreeable because they're excellent hosts and it's a lot of fun. But I know when the screenplay leaves my hands, it's going to be rewritten — and who knows what's gonna hit the screen? I know where I stand. I have a ball, but it's foolish to get carried away.

I don't see them as sucking out our life's blood. I think Hollywood's enthusiasm is like a high wind that goes up for a long time and people party a little too hard.

**EISNER:** That's an important point. We just finished saying that comics artists feel that their success in this field is when they take a strip and make a movie of it — then they've "arrived." But now we've seen a lot of creators who had movies made of their comic strips, but they're nowhere. I know of one guy who had a movie made of his comics and the property he created is literally dead; it's not even being published anymore.

**MILLER:** When you're dealing with something that you've created, be very protective. If you love it, if it's still an alive and ongoing thing ...

In an unprecedented departure for the film industry, Robert Rodriguez invited Miller to co-direct *Sin City*. Here, the artist poses with actress Jaime King, who plays Goldie, a character from *Sin City: The Hard Goodbye*. *Photo courtesy of Dimension Films.*

**The cover of *Dark Horse Presents* #62, in which the conclusion of *Sin City: The Hard Goodbye* was published. © 1992 Frank Miller, Inc.**

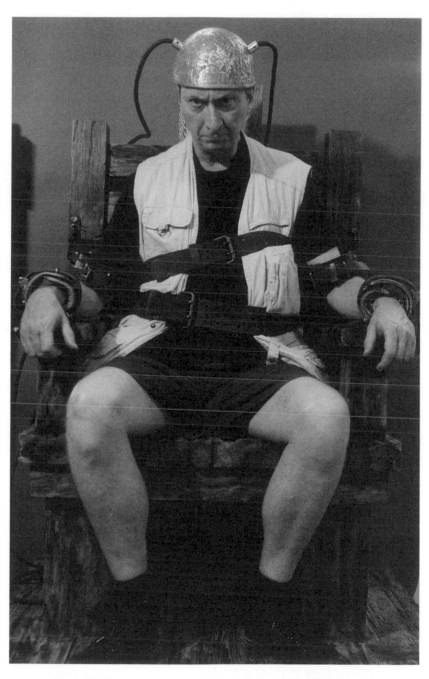

**Miller mimicking his own artwork, on the set of *Frank Miller's Sin City*.**
*Photo courtesy of Dimension Films.*

**EISNER:**  Well, you have to resist the temptation of having a movie made …

**MILLER:**  What I'm getting at is I've noticed many artists have sold the movie rights, gotten involved with Hollywood, and then their own enthusiasm for the original property tends to vanish and they never go back [to their comic].  So understand: that is a concern.

**EISNER:**  I agree that Hollywood represents, to a lot of creators, the ultimate goal for any comic strip that's created.  It also is the hope of any novelist being published today.

**MILLER:**  I'm just saying the thing that bothers me most is that comic books think that Hollywood is a big step "up."  When I first got hired to write a movie I did not consider it a step up.

For all my sarcasm I can understand completely why it would be fun to do a comic, then get the money and have somebody who really wanted to do it make a movie of the comic.  I can see that being a ball.

**EISNER:**  It's a ball — but intellectually?  When you've just written *Sin City*, do you feel an intellectual need, an emotional need, to have a movie made of that?

**MILLER:**  No.  I've turned down a lot of offers.  But I think it might be something I do once I've decided that I'm done with *Sin City*.

**EISNER:**  Why would you want to do it then?

**MILLER:**  It would probably be for fun and money.

**EISNER:**  Money, yes.  I can understand money.  Fun?  Fun, I think you're …

**MILLER:**  I just am trying to be clear that I don't think we can turn our backs on Hollywood.

**EISNER:** What happens when Hollywood gets *Sin City*? They're going to make a movie that's a hell of a lot different than what *Sin City* is when you're doing it.

**MILLER:** Technologies are changing, so who knows?

**EISNER:** Aside from technology, I'm talking about the intellectual content.

**MILLER:** Who knows? There's animation that can be done differently now, and that's just exploding. Who knows if it would even go through Hollywood?

**EISNER:** Frank, you and I are talking about different things. You're talking about technology, and I'm talking about an intellectual impulse here. The feeling you have ... and maybe you don't have any feeling for *Sin City*.

**MILLER:** I just told you that I've turned down offers because I'm too *close* to it! It's too precious, and I don't want ...

**EISNER:** You just said it. Too precious. I like that. It's precious to you. You don't want to see it warped into a movie at this time, or any time. Later on, maybe, there might be a point at which you feel you're no longer interested in this story, and if Hollywood takes it and distorts it ...

**MILLER:** I was the one who went on this tirade about running over to Hollywood. I know what compromises are involved. I was just saying I don't condemn anyone for wanting to go in that direction, because it's a very exciting field. Just know what you're getting yourself into. Be smart.

# 28.·····

# MANAGING
# YOUR CAREER

**EISNER:** What strategy would you recommend for a young cartoonist coming into the field today?

**MILLER:** I can only talk about what worked for me, and one method is to establish yourself in comics with work-for-hire, get the name, and then parlay that into a place in the field.

**EISNER:** You're saying to a young writer, first become Ernest Hemingway, then worry about the deal you make?

**MILLER:** No. I'm saying do a bunch of work-for-hire, get the largest possible audience, and then ...

**EISNER:** See, I would say that perhaps the best way we can answer that is to say you have to have behind you a large body of things that you want to say and develop later when you've reached the point when you no longer have to do pencilling or inking for an outfit. Then, when you don't need a day job, think about owning your work.

**MILLER:** Getting there was a transition period for me, because I went from doing work-for-hire stuff to writing new stuff that other people would co-own; then finally I made the full-on commitment to the first book that I ever did completely from top to bottom, including the lettering and everything, and it was a perfect stake in the course of my career. I knew that I wanted to bring back crime comics; that's what I'd always wanted to do. So I finally got to do the work I wanted when I first brought my portfolio to New York.

**EISNER:** That was logical. You went through a whole number of stages, which is what most young cartoonists will have to do. They have to walk the same rocky road that you walked on: starting off by doing inking or pencilling for a major house until they reach a point where they develop a self-confidence. If they have no more to say, no inventory of things that they want to do, then they might remain inking for the rest of their lives. But if they have something more and can go a year without any income …

**MILLER:** The other thing — and I can't tell you anything but what worked for me — but there are publishers who will take unknowns and publish them. The sacrifice is that you won't be paid much at all, and you won't get the exposure that you get on an established property.

**EISNER:** That's the marvelous thing about the field today. There are twenty or thirty small publishers. There's a place today for a young person to go. He's been doing pencilling or inking for a major publishing house and says, "God, I'm tired of doing this. I have some ideas. I think I'd like to bring back a Dashiell Hammett-type crime story." So he does his day job and saves enough money to spend a year doing this thing; he does it, gives it to a publisher, the guy publishes two thousand copies of this thing, and he's got a book out there. He hasn't made any money from it, but he's got a book out there. It raises his status, in my opinion. When he goes back to Marvel or DC with a book that he's published, they look at him differently.

> ## "The Internet is gonna play some kind of role. It is a Tower of Babel, but it allows access to an awful lot of eyes. It's airplay."

**MILLER:** Yeah. One thing I've got to mention that I do think is relevant in all of this is that I'm sure the Internet is gonna play some kind of role. It is a Tower of Babel, but it allows access to an awful lot of eyes. It's airplay. The cartoonists will make no money, but people will see [their work]. It's a way to get your stuff out there, and it's risky only in that everybody else can do it at the same time and most of the stuff out there's gonna be pretty horrible. But despite that, I do think the Internet is gonna be a way for people to show what they've got. Comics are changing so much that we have no idea exactly what kind of thing is coming up.

**EISNER:** It won't be one thing; it'll be a whole business.

**MILLER:** Yeah, it has to be.

**EISNER:** There'll be my kind of thing, your kind of thing, Chris Ware's kind of thing, the guy who's doing Pimple-Man, whatever the case. There are a lot of things that have survived. Look at *Zippy the Pinhead*. That thing has survived, to my amazement. I'm astonished to see it regarded

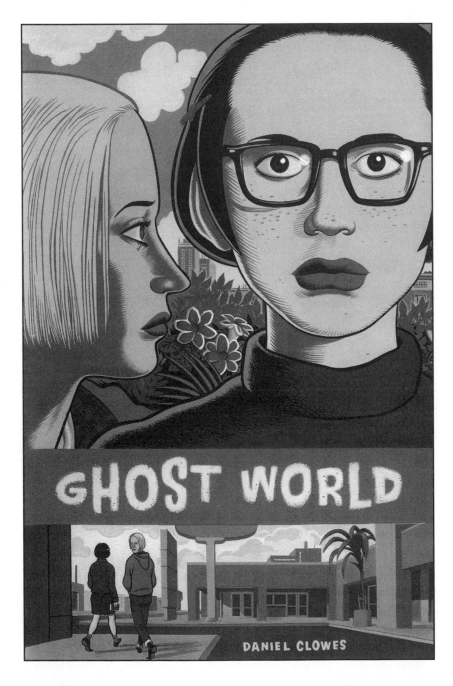

**In addition to much critical acclaim in the comics field, Dan Clowes's** *Ghost World* **also went on to become a successful film.** © *1997 Daniel Clowes*

as a viable commercial property *[Miller laughs]*. I don't know how it got there. But the point is that there's room for all these different kinds of things.

This is what I think is happening to the field: I think the field is breaking into small, specialized segments.

**MILLER:** If so, then I'll get my wish and we'll move closer to traditional publishing. Comics will be a way stories are told, rather than a self-defined genre.

**EISNER:** Well, Pantheon is beginning to do that now. Since they published Chris Ware and discovered there's money to be made ...

From its beginnings in underground comix, Bill Griffith's *Zippy the Pinhead* has gone on to become a "viable commercial property" as a newspaper comics strip. © *1980 Bill Griffith*

**MILLER:** Yeah, and *Ghost World* did well. This is vital because the direct market is missing a lot of people. This is why I worry about the questions here. Asking me to tell what I did 25 years ago coming in ... it was a vastly different field. I came in and did the only work I could get. I don't know how I'd enter the field right now. It's so changed that it might be a good time to just come in brash and say, "This is who I am and what I do, and I'm not gonna waste a day of my career doing anything else."

# 29.⋯⋯

# THE FUTURE

*After a long day at the studio, Miller and Eisner return to Will's house for a nightcap and a final conversation by the pool.*

**MILLER:** One of the most frequently asked questions is: Where are things going? You've been here from the beginning, Will. Where do you think things are going?

**EISNER:** First of all, the idea of telling stories with images will remain; in whatever transmission method, that will remain. If print disappears completely, which I don't think will happen, there will still be the technology that transmits stories told by pictures. To me, comics is a way of telling a story. It's a way of writing. It's a language.

⋯⋯⋯⋯⋯⋯⋯⋯⋯⋯⋯⋯⋯⋯⋯⋯

**Opposite: Telling stories with pictures has a vast history and a vast future, according to Eisner. From *Graphic Storytelling*. © 1995 Will Eisner**

When you ask where this medium of comics is going ... who the hell knows where the industry is going?  The one thing I do know is that for a long time to come, well into the future, the business of telling stories with imagery is going to remain with us.  In fact, the use of imagery as a storytelling device will probably expand, because society is moving into an era in which time is of the essence and we must tell a story quickly.  The reader doesn't have time to sit down and read a whole text the way he did at one time.  Now he wants to get the story quickly. Furthermore, readers will become more sophisticated.  What do you think, Frank?

> **"We could have something so brand-new happening that we can't even imagine its shape."**

**MILLER:**  My best guess is that the bookstores are key at this point. We're dealing with a medium that has to be read, and Americans don't read.  We've got to become part of the publishing industry in a meaningful way.  And I want to see the end of comic book sections in bookstores and see us in all the relevant places.

**EISNER:**  So what you're saying is that the major book publishing business would begin to encompass this medium.

**MILLER:**  Yeah, and it seems to have started.

**EISNER:**  So comic book stores will disappear?

**MILLER:**  No, I don't think the comic book stores will disappear.  I think, like everything else, things seem to find a better purpose when they're faced with a new technology.  And I can see the comics shop turn into a place that's like a coffee shop *cum* comics shop *cum* music store. It would accommodate the natural way that devoted fans like to congregate. The comics shops will become a different kind of place.

**EISNER:** You're talking about market; I'm talking about a medium.

**MILLER:** You said I suggested comics shops were going to disappear, so I was answering that. Getting back to the medium, I just know that we've gotta get *out* there. I guess my main goal is that I want to see *Sin City* next to Mickey Spillane, rather than next to *Spawn*.

**EISNER:** I don't blame you *[chuckles]*. I'm saying that, to me, the medium is not the comic book sitting next to *Spawn*; the medium is not the comic book we see today. To me, the medium is the business of communicating stories with images, the intelligent combine of words and images. This is what we all know very well. I see comics as a medium; I don't see it as something being printed on paper, or necessarily done on the Internet, or whatever the case may be. I see it as a marketable item in itself, and that's the thing that I think will survive regardless of how it's distributed: the fact that this medium is valid, and essential, and worthwhile, and delivers. There will be an economic structure to support it, because people will be willing to pay for it.

> "As creatures, we need to communicate, and communicating with images will endure."

**MILLER:** Also, I think we may be underestimating the people who are starting to come in now. We could have a 21st-century underground movement that we couldn't have even imagined coming in before. We could have something so brand-new happening that we can't even imagine

**Comic-Con International: San Diego had an estimated attendance of 76,000 people in 2003.** *Photo by Jackie Estrada.*

its shape.  I don't know enough about what's going on, but I know it could be a lot different and hit us from a lot of different directions.

**EISNER:**   Everything I've said so far is based on the fact that I've sidestepped the requirement to imagine the shape of the things to come. I'm talking about the fact that there is a basic method of communication, based on the use of images, that will survive.  How it's transmitted is something that I can't predict, and nobody really is able to predict that. No one in 1925 could predict that there would even be comic books!

I can tell you now, sitting here, I'm still astonished over the fact that there's such a thing as a comics convention.  I couldn't imagine it in 1938 when I started Eisner & Iger.  I didn't dream that there would someday be conventions with thousands of people attending and comic books being traded.  It didn't even occur to me.  I don't know what will happen, but I'll tell you that, as creatures, we need to communicate, and communicating with images will endure.

# 30. .....
# LEGACY

**MILLER:** How do you feel about your career when you look back on it?

**EISNER:** I feel a bit like Horatio Alger. I worked hard. I didn't marry the boss's daughter, but I worked hard, kept my nose clean, did the right thing, saved my money, and ultimately wound up being the chairman of the board. No regrets. What about you?

**MILLER:** My work's been a lot of fun. Mostly I see it all as a terrific opportunity to do something that I really want to do in a field that's in many ways underdeveloped. It's been a combination of persistence and good fortune, I guess, that I get to do exactly what I want to do. And it's still an achievable dream. I think we're in for another wave that'll be unlike anything we've ever seen.

..............................................................................................

**Opposite: Looking back on a lifetime spent in comics. From *To the Heart of the Storm*. © 1991 Will Eisner**

**EISNER:** For a youngster who's coming along now and walking around with a black portfolio, I think it happens faster. You've got a guy who's 28 years old, or even younger, who walks in and develops a comic that gets picked up by a major house, and suddenly he's a star, he's winning an award, he's flying high, making money …

**MILLER:** Also, the stylistic restrictions on comics are far fewer than they used to be. It's only recently that the "house style," which I used to ridicule, has become one choice among many.

**EISNER:** That's the wonderful thing about this business: it attracts creative people. People are inventing ways to enjoy this sequential arrangement of images to tell stories.

> "It was one thing to sell *The Spirit* to a newspaper syndicate, but I had to be able to deliver. Big difference. My achievement was not in selling it; my achievement was in delivering."

**MILLER:** Getting back to how to break into comics, it's probably a mistake even to contemplate using my model — my strategy for getting to this position is out of date, I'm sure. This business is vastly transformed from when I entered.

**EISNER:** Oh, yeah. In this society, we are seeing young people who just got out of college walk into a brokerage house and come home millionaires in sixty days. In comics, you see young artists can become success stories overnight, very easily. I can see a young guy coming out of SPX walk into a publishing house and overnight become a sensation.

He can be a big star in a major publishing house, and by the time he's 23 years old he's worth several million dollars, he's lionized on radio, and the first thing was this comic book.

**MILLER:** And then he'll squander it all on a terrible substance abuse problem *[laughter]*!

**EISNER:** That will happen because he won't have had the years of experience to know what to do with money. Because money came surprisingly easily, and that's something else again. But what we're talking about is the so-called Horatio Alger concept. The Horatio Alger idea no longer works. My students used to say to me, "Are you telling me to go out there and get a job doing paste-ups and mechanicals? I want to do *New Yorker* covers right away!" As a matter of fact, *The New Yorker* might buy one of their covers for all I know, but that would be just a fluke! The formulas that are being posed here may no longer be really valid or usable. They're practical, they're realistic, and one might want to be prepared to go the same route. That route will still be there. It may take until you're forty years old to establish yourself, or you might be nineteen years old and a star. These are things that happen along the way, but you've got to be there, and you must be able to deliver. It was one thing to sell *The Spirit* to a newspaper syndicate, but I had to be able to deliver. Big difference. My achievement was not in selling it; my achievement was in delivering.

**MILLER:** You've said that when you came back and did *A Contract with God*, it felt like you were stepping back from outer space.

**EISNER:** Well, yeah. The world was different. I felt like Rip Van Winkle. I felt things were different. Young kids were running around doing things, and comics were selling in comic book stores, which I'd never seen before. I had been in touch with the field, I knew what had been going on over the years, but I hadn't realized that coming back into the field, getting involved in it myself again, was going to be so different.

*Photo by Charles Brownstein.*

Comic book stores! Remember, when I started, there were no comic book stores. The newsstands were occupied by guys with busted noses and dead cigars.

**MILLER:** And the publishing houses were, too!

**EISNER:** The publishers were weird characters. One old publisher was crazy. There was a small publisher who had no teeth, and he would chew on old pieces of paper while he talked to you and was buying comic books from you. This was a publisher!

**MILLER:** I'll work for *him*!

**EISNER:** It was a totally different world. I came back, and there were Marvel and DC and comic book stores and conventions. You have to think about the difference. It was not stunning, but it was exciting to me. It was a new world.

**MILLER:** I think of that period a bit like the dark ages, where something was kept alive against the odds. The direct market sort of helped the people who still wanted comics, and gave them a way to get them and a profitable way to produce them.

**EISNER:** Nobody in my time thought the field had a future! We didn't even think of it as a *field*. We thought comic book publishers were a source of business — maybe they'd be around, maybe they wouldn't. We'd seen magazines die. Nobody thought the *Saturday Evening Post* would die, but it did, and something else replaced it. So the world [of comics] is different now, and it was different when I came back. But I had something else in mind. I came back with a very practical plan. In 1974 or '75 when I started *A Contract with God* — it wasn't until 1978 that it got published — I reasoned that the fourteen- and fifteen-year-old guys whom I was writing to in 1938, '39, and '40 would now be 35 or forty years old, and I couldn't believe that they would continue to be reading Superman stories. I reasoned that they had to be wanting something else, something more serious.

**MILLER:** Rather than Rip Van Winkle, maybe you felt like the Connecticut Yankee in King Arthur's Court. Because your picture was so forward-looking.

**EISNER:** That's a better analogy. My reasoning was very practical. On the other hand, I felt there was something that I had to do that I hadn't yet done.

It was a totally different time. First of all, the method of printing books had changed. Comic books were coming out in full color. People like your wife Lynn [Varley] were making full color paintings. The Spanish artists were coming in with watercolor and even oil paintings and printing them in comics. That was inconceivable where I came from.

**MILLER:** Forbidden Planet [a London-based comics retail chain] had opened in New York, bringing the entire world of comics to that building.

**EISNER:** That's right. It was a huge place.

**MILLER:** It was a mecca back then.

**EISNER:** Oh, yes. But the big thing to me was the conventions. I had never in my life ever dreamed that there would be conventions. One of Seuling's conventions at the Commodore Hotel on 42nd Street [in New York] really blew me away.

**MILLER:** Those early conventions felt like meetings of a secret tribe — one that was threatened and trying to stay alive.

**EISNER:** It was a cult kind of thing.

**MILLER:** There was a sense of such peril and "They all hate us, but we still love this and are sticking to it."

What is your feeling about posterity, and the legacy you're leaving?

**EISNER:** Starting with posterity, we're all under a sentence of death. I've got a lot to do before I go …

**MILLER:** And you ain't cleaning the sheets before you leave.

**EISNER:** No, I'm not. But as far as leaving a legacy, I want to be remembered for having cut a path in the woods. That's all I can claim. The rest of it is what anybody else will say. But I can't even say I was the first. If anybody followed me, if I was right or I was wrong, that's irrelevant. History will decide whether I was right or wrong. I did something I believed in. I believe strongly that this medium is capable of subject matter well beyond the business of pursuit and vengeance or two mutants trashing each other. If I helped prove that, then that's all I can ask for. That applause will last for a few years after I'm gone, and then it'll fade into history.

**MILLER:** You've got a dark side. And I'm not gonna argue with you over a subject that's as personal as that, but I think you will be remembered much more intensely.

**EISNER:** Great.

**MILLER:** But, meanwhile, don't hurry!

**EISNER:** No, I've still got a lot of miles to go. As far as the body of work is concerned, there's still a lot undone. But the body of work is nothing more than evidence.

> "People who have small egos can't do this kind of stuff. It requires not just an idea, but a confidence in yourself that the idea is worth pursuing, book by book, for a year of your life or so."

**MILLER:** That's a beautiful sentiment. The body of work is basically the evidence of a very long camping trip *[Eisner laughs]*.

**EISNER:** That's right. I'm glad to hear me getting credit for having cut new ground. That's all that you can ask.

**MILLER:** In your career, perhaps in any person's career, there's so much talk about art and commerce and so on, there are two things that are inextricably linked at certain points. The reason I keep coming back to the importance of *A Contract with God* is because that was a very, very audacious move on your part. On many levels you were already adored for work you'd done a long time before, but mainly the statement

**Beginners in the comics field need to be prepared for rejection, says Eisner.
From *AutobioGraphix*.  © 2003 Will Eisner**

*Contract with God* made is that you painted a picture of where to go. You did that and handed us a map, too.

**EISNER:** And we can go beyond what I did. Sure, I did something good, but you guys have been doing great stuff, and I think you can go beyond this. To be able to do that in a lifetime is no mean thing. I'm not modest or underestimating what I think I did. Also, one has to have an eternal belief in one's self that enables you to do a thing like that.

**MILLER:** People who have small egos can't do this kind of stuff. It requires not just an idea, but a confidence in yourself that the idea is worth pursuing, book by book, for a year of your life or so.

**EISNER:** I used to tell students, "Look, if you want to go into this field, one thing you've got to be prepared for is rejection. You'll bring your work into the studio one day, and the editor'll look at it and say, 'Don't take this personally, but this is the lousiest crap I've ever seen.'"

**MILLER:** My favorite ever was: "Where are you from?" My answer was "Vermont." He said, "Go home." That was about the rudest rejection I ever got. He was a perfectly nice guy.

**EISNER:** Rejection is very much a part of this business. One of the reasons why artists make deals that they're sorry for later is fear of rejection. Another part of this is the willingness to do something, even though all the evidence you have in hand tells you it's going to be an unrequited action, but you say you're going to do it because you believe that you're right. *A Contract with God* was done in response to two very strong elements in my makeup. One is a practical recognition of the fact that there was going to be an audience for this: I will put my stake in the ground and they will come. The other thing I believed is that there were things I wanted to say, wanted to do yet, that I needed to get done. I didn't necessarily think it would be fun — a word you use frequently. I felt this was something that needed to be done to satisfy my own sensibilities. That's my reason. Yours?

In *Fagin the Jew*, Eisner makes a strong statement against ethnic stereotyping — in particular, against anti-Semitism — in life and in literature.
© 2003 Will Eisner

**MILLER:** That's a tough act to follow.

**EISNER:** Hey, listen, you've got a way to go yet, man. I'm well into the woods; you're just halfway in. Where do you think you want to be thirty years from now? The eighty-year-old Frank Miller, where will you be? Okay, you'll be a multimillionaire at eighty, fine. You'll own a lot of property, maybe you'll even own a major controlling interest of a publishing company. How do you want to see yourself?

> **"I want to be remembered for having cut a path in the woods. That's all I can claim. The rest of it is what anybody else will say."**

**MILLER:** I really most want to remain a vital force in the field and be a part of the changes that are coming. I don't know where it's going. I don't know where my own work is going. I've got a lot of ideas and I'm pursuing them, of course, but most of all I want to stay engaged with it as an artist.

**EISNER:** That's fair enough. That's as good an ambition as anybody can have, in my opinion. I think right now we're at a turning point. This is a turning point in the history of this medium. That's why when we talk about where this medium is going, I don't think it'll disappear. There will be great people coming into this medium, people who can write, who have something to say, and who are not interested necessarily in the fun — doing an exciting adventure story or a cops-and-robbers story or whatever they do. They're interested in having something serious to say. That's what I'm hoping to do now with *Fagin* and with all my work. I'm hoping to make a statement that maybe hasn't been fully considered up to now. If it works, then I'm off in a new direction.

## GRAPHIC NOVELS BY WILL EISNER

The Building
City People Notebook
A Contract with God
The Dreamer
Dropsie Avenue: The Neighborhood
Fagin the Jew
A Family Matter
Invisible People
Last Day in Vietnam
A Life Force
Life on Another Planet
Minor Miracles
The Name of the Game
New York: The Big City
The Plot: The Secret Story of the Protocols of the Elders of Zion
The Spirit Archives
To the Heart of the Storm
Will Eisner Reader

# GRAPHIC NOVELS BY FRANK MILLER

Daredevil Visionaries: Frank Miller, vols. 1-3
Sin City, vol. 1: The Hard Goodbye
Sin City, vol. 2: A Dame to Kill For
Sin City, vol. 3: The Big Fat Kill
Sin City, vol. 4: That Yellow Bastard
Sin City, vol. 5: Family Values
Sin City, vol. 6: Booze, Broads, & Bullets
Sin City, vol. 7: Hell and Back

*with Lynn Varley*
300
Batman: The Dark Knight Returns
Batman: The Dark Knight Strikes Again
Elektra Lives Again
Ronin

*with Geof Darrow*
The Big Guy and Rusty the Boy Robot
Hard Boiled

*with Dave Gibbons*
Give Me Liberty
Martha Washington Goes to War
Martha Washington Saves the World

*with David Mazzucchelli*
Batman: Year One

*with John Romita, Jr.*
Daredevil: Man without Fear

*with Bill Sienkiewicz*
Elektra: Assassin

# SUGGESTIONS FOR FURTHER READING

Andelman, Bob. *Will Eisner: A Spirited Life.* Milwaukie, OR: M Press, 2005.

Couch, N.C. Christopher, and Weiner, Stephen. *The Will Eisner Companion.* New York, NY: DC Comics, 2004.

Duin, Steve, and Richardson, Mike. *Comics: Between the Panels.* Milwaukie, OR: Dark Horse Comics, 1998.

Eisner, Will. *Comics & Sequential Art.* Tamarac, FL: Poorhouse Press, 1985.

—. *Graphic Storytelling.* Tamarac, FL: Poorhouse Press, 1996.

—. *The Will Eisner Sketchbook.* Milwaukie, OR: Dark Horse Books, 2004.

Feiffer, Jules. *The Great Comic Book Heroes.* New York: The Dial Press, 1956.

Greenberger, Robert. *Will Eisner.* New York: Rosen Publishing Group, 2005.

Groth, Gary, and Fiore, Robert, eds. *The New Comics.* New York: Berkley Books, 1988.

Harvey, Robert C. *The Art of the Comic Book: An Aesthetic History.* Jackson: University Press of Mississippi, 1996.

—, ed. *Milton Caniff: Conversations.* Jackson: University Press of Mississippi, 2002.

Inge, M. Thomas. *Comics as Culture.* Jackson: University Press of Mississippi, 1990.

# ACKNOWLEDGMENTS

This book was a few years in the making.

After Frank Miller and Charles Brownstein flew south to spend that May 2002 weekend in Florida with Will Eisner, the resulting hours and hours of interview tapes were painstakingly transcribed, organized, and edited by Charles. The manuscript then underwent a preliminary edit at my end, with further copyedits by both Will and Frank. Next, Charles undertook the laborious task of another edit, culling pull quotes along the way as well as choosing appropriate illustrations and photos. I provided the final edit — the final several edits, actually — selecting even more illustrations; writing captions and footnotes; compiling bibliographies; hounding Will and Frank and Denis Kitchen, and comics historian R.C. Harvey, for last-minute information; and overseeing Cary Grazzini's meticulous typesetting and design, and retypesetting and redesign.

Thanks are due to all of the above as well as to Jim Kuhoric of Diamond Comic Distributors for providing materials necessary for scanning and to Aaron Fuller for reading the manuscript and offering editorial feedback.

Sadly, Will passed away just a few months before this book could finally see print, but I remain especially and eternally grateful to him and to Frank for their commitment to the project. All insights contained herein are theirs. Any errors are mine.

— Diana Schutz

Jones, Gerry. *Men of Tomorrow: Geeks, Gangsters, and the Birth of the Comic Book.* New York, NY: Basic Books, 2004.

Lupoff, Dick, and Thompson, Don, eds. *All in Color for a Dime.* New York: Ace Books, 1970.

—, eds. *The Comic-Book Book.* New Rochelle, NY: Arlington House, 1973.

McCloud, Scott. *Reinventing Comics.* New York: Paradox Press, 2000.

—. *Understanding Comics.* Northampton, MA: Tundra Publishing, 1993.

Miller, Frank. *The Art of Sin City.* Milwaukie, OR: Dark Horse Comics, 2002.

Robbins, Trina. *The Great Women Cartoonists.* New York: Watson-Guptill Publications, 2001.

Rosenkranz, Patrick. *Rebel Visions: The Underground Comix Revolution 1963-1975.* Seattle: Fantagraphics Books, 2002.

Schutz, Diana, and Kitchen, Denis, eds. *Will Eisner's Shop Talk.* Milwaukie, OR: Dark Horse Comics, 2001.

Talon, Durwin S. *Panel Discussions.* Raleigh, NC: TwoMorrows Publishing, 2003.

Wiater, Stanley, and Bissette, Stephen R., eds. *Comics Book Rebels: Conversations with the Creators of the New Comics.* New York: Donald I. Fine, 1993.

Witek, Joseph. *Comic Books as History: The Narrative Art of Jack Jackson, Art Spiegelman, and Harvey Pekar.* Jackson: University Press of Mississippi, 1989.